GOLF'S
ED ZONE CHALLENGE

Breakthrough System to Track and Improve Your Short Game
And Significantly Lower Your Score

Charlie King
and
Rob Akins

P9-ASF-138

Athlon® Sports™

AMERICA'S PREMIER SPORTS ANNUALS

WILLISTON PARK PUBLIC LIBRARY

Copyright © 2005 by Athlon Sports Communications, Inc.

No part of this publication may be reproduced, stored in a retrieval system, or transmitted, in any form by any means, electronic, mechanical, photocopying, or otherwise, without the prior written permission of the publisher, Triumph Books, 601 S. LaSalle St., Suite 500, Chicago, Illinois 60605.

This book is available in quantity at special discounts for your group or organization. For further information, contact:

Triumph Books
601 South LaSalle Street
Suite 500
Chicago, Illinois 60605
(312) 939-3330
Fax (312) 663-3557

Printed in Hong Kong
ISBN-13: 978-1-57243-720-3
ISBN-10: 1-57243-720-0

Editor: Rob Doster
Photographer/Photo Editor: Tim Clark
Design: Tom Davis

Photo credits:
Steve Schaefer/AFP/Getty Images (p.2); David Cannon/Getty Images (pp.6–7, 16); Tony Roberts/Corbis (p.10); Focus on Sport/Getty Images (p.23); Brian Ebner/Optic Nerve (p.24)
All other photos by Tim Clark/Athlon Sports

Instruction photos taken at Tom Watson's Independence Course at Reunion Resort and Club of Orlando

Contents

About the Authors

Charlie King is recognized by Golf Magazine as one of America's Top 100 golf instructors. An experienced "pro's pro" and currently the PGA Teaching Professional at Nantucket (Mass.) Golf Club, Charlie formerly ran the large teaching operation at PGA National, sharing his knowledge with other teaching professionals, as well as a wide array of golfers of every ability level. His teaching approach incorporates golf fitness and mental performance segments along with swing instruction.

Rob Akins of Germantown, Tenn., has been channeling his passion for golf into teaching since he was age 16. His pupils include childhood friend and 2001 PGA Champion David Toms, eight-time Tour winner Loren Roberts, and David Gossett, the 1999 U.S. Amateur Champion. Rob, who is a member of both *Golf Magazine*'s Top 100 and *Golf Digest*'s Top 50 Teachers, also counts basketball legend Jerry West among his students.

Dedicated to the memory of Norman Akins, father of Rob Akins

Acknowledgments

We all are influenced in our careers by certain coaches. My ideas for this book have been influenced by (in no particular order):

Rob Akins - My co-author is the most influential and unique golf instructor I have met. He has been a great partner on this project and puts his heart and soul into teaching daily.

Coach Conrad Rehling - He impressed upon me the importance of measurements through skills tests. He is a great friend and colleague and a great man.

PGA Professional Jerry Tucker - Jerry's idea to handicap short games was a huge step forward for showing a golfer where they stand. I heard about it at the 1990 PGA Teaching and Coaching Summit and integrated it into my teaching.

PGA Professional Brad Turner - We worked on the program together at the Golf Academy of the South to integrate these principles with, I must say modestly, great success. One of the best short games I have ever seen.

Dr. Rick Jensen - Rick is the most practical Sports Psychologist I have met or heard. He explained to me how to set up a program for a motor skill like golf and it has made a huge difference.

PGA Professional Craig Shankland - His energy and example have influenced my teaching and I am honored to call him my friend.

Tony Robbins - His life coaching ideas are Life 101 for me. I have never seen a more committed coach.

Bill Phillips - His book Body-for-Life sparked an idea 5 years ago for how to motivate in golf.

I want to thank:
- My wife Julie for her love and support, my daughter Kathryn for her creativity and my son Brian for his sense of humor.
- The people at Athlon Sports Communications for the professional manner in which this project has been handled. Especially Rob Doster for being point man and editor extraordinaire.
- Bill Settle for the energy and vision he has shown daily to making the Red Zone Challenge a reality.
- Triumph Books for believing in this book.
- Brian Candela, Scotty Griffin, Kevin Walker and Carroll Clark for the almost daily 'book talk' sessions.

-Charlie King

I want to thank:
- My wife Deborah and sons Matthew, Heath and Lake.
- My students for their desire to learn and to become the best they can be.
- Charlie King, for his tireless efforts to make the Red Zone become a reality.

-Rob Akins

WHEN I STOOD ON THE

72nd hole of the 2001 PGA Championship at Atlanta Athletic Club, I was faced with the most important decision of my career. I was one stroke ahead of Phil Mickelson and needed a par to earn my first major championship - or, at the very least, to clinch a spot in a playoff should Phil make birdie. But I had a dilemma. I had driven the ball into the first cut of rough on the 490-yard par-4 18th hole and was facing a tough second shot into a green guarded by water front and left.

It was then that I recalled the hours of work that I had put into my short game with my teacher, Rob Akins. I was so confident in my short game that I knew if I laid up, I could get up and down for that all-important par.

And that's exactly what happened. Instead of trying to play the hero and pull off a miraculous 5-wood shot to the green, I placed the burden on my wedge and my putter to take me to my first major. After laying up, I stuck my wedge shot 12 feet from the hole, then watched as Phil left his birdie putt short. As I stood over that 12-footer, the long hours I had spent on practice greens from Louisiana to California seemed like the best time I had ever spent. Halfway there, I knew the putt was pure.

After that story, I don't think I need to tell you the level of importance I place on the short game. Rob and his co-author, Charlie King, understand exactly what I am talking about.

Rob and I grew up together in Shreveport, Louisiana, where we played junior golf against one another. It was then, after I had so thoroughly whipped him, that he decided his real future was in teaching, not playing.

Every student - myself included - who has ever benefited from Rob's teaching will tell you that that was the best decision he ever made. After you read this book. I have no doubt that you will agree.

"Rob and Charlie have created a simple plan for short game improvement that will take your game to a new level"

Rob and I began our student-teacher relationship in 1994, when I was a young, aspiring pro with a lot to learn. In 1996, Rob became my primary, full-time swing coach, and the results speak for themselves. Over these last eight-plus years, I have been fortunate enough to play consistent, championship-level golf, and I owe much of my success to Rob's solid teaching principles, his infectious passion for the game and his unmatched motivational skills.

Now, you can benefit from those very same things. The drills, games and information that Rob and I use in our short game practice sessions are now available to you in this innovative book.

Rob and Charlie have created a simple plan for short game improvement that will take your game to a new level. Their "Red Zone" drills, their motivational techniques and their simple, direct approach to teaching will have you playing your best golf from 100 yards and in.

Taking a lesson with either Rob or Charlie can require months to schedule, but you can start learning from them today. By following the simple program they lay out in this book, you can start posting the best scores of your life.

You may not win a major, but I can guarantee that Rob and Charlie will help you enjoy the game more than you ever have.

- David Toms

1

THE
ATHLON
RED ZONE

FIRST THINGS FIRST—

you're probably asking yourself what the Red Zone has to do with golf. That term is most familiar to football fans, who know the Red Zone as that space on the football field from the 20-yard line to the end zone. It's where games are won and lost.

Fans live and die with the Red Zone proficiency of their favorite teams. How many times have you heard a comment like this: "We've moved it all day long between the 20s, but we can't score when we get close." It's absolutely critical for teams to take advantage of their Red Zone opportunities — scoring a touchdown, or at worst, a field goal — if they want to win games. (If you're not a football fan, just work with us on this.)

Guess what? In a very real sense, golf is no different. We've simply borrowed a term from football and applied it to that space on a golf course — 100 yards from the green and in — where, just like in football, you can make the biggest impact on your score.

You want to be better at golf — otherwise, you wouldn't have bought this book. In our combined 35 years of teaching golf, we have never met a person who didn't want to get better. Our daily lessons with golfers of all skill levels tell us that golfers are searching for that magic cure, for that secret formula that results in better golf.

And among all the golfers we've encountered, we have yet to meet one who doesn't know how important the short game is. Yet we very rarely see golfers working on the short game as hard as the full swing. Apparently, cranking out a 275-yard drive is more fun than hitting a wedge shot stiff, executing a deft chip shot or holing a 10-foot putt.

But we contend that those wedges, chips and putts are more important to your score than a booming long game.

Here's our guarantee: If you work on your short game — on your "Red Zone" skills — you'll see your scores improve.

Think of golf's Red Zone this way. Hole the ball out or get up and down in two shots, and you have scored a touchdown. Get up and down in three shots and you have kicked a field goal. Taking four

or more to get down from 100 yards and in? Well, that's like missing a field goal, or worse, throwing an interception and having it returned for a touchdown.

One more football analogy: You've certainly heard it said that defense wins championships. In golf, think of the full swing as your flashy offense and the short game as your championship-winning defense.

It's that important.

We have heard all the objections: "I'll start caring about the short game as soon as you can get me on or near the green in regulation. I don't care about getting up and down for a 10."

Those objections are understandable. The full swing and the long game are vitally important. But we don't think players fully appreciate the impact that Red Zone improvement can have on their enjoyment of the game.

> "Think of the full swing as your flashy offense and the short game as your championship-winning defense."

We had a common desire to do something about this problem. So we did, and we're thrilled with the results. We believe we've created a program that golf has never seen, one that combines motivation to improve your short game with easy-to-follow steps for getting there.

We want you to take the Athlon Red Zone Challenge that's presented in the pages that follow. By taking our simple test, giving yourself a short game handicap and following our 12-week program, you'll watch your scores plummet.

Before you start, go to **www.athlonsports.com** to get details about entering our national contest. We are going to put our money where our mouth is. We want you to be motivated to do this and to follow it through to its ultimate conclusion.

And here's a bonus: The habits you will learn in this book for pitching and chipping will help the full swing!

The ultimate Red Zone moment: Larry Mize chips in to beat Greg Norman at the 1987 Masters.

If you came to us on the lesson tee, we would look you in the eye and say, "We challenge you to see what your potential is. No excuses." We're doing the same thing with this book.

Unlike many golf teaching programs — some of which you may be intimately familiar with — we're not going to give you a few tips or gimmicks and send you on your way. We are going to arm you with the tools you absolutely need to succeed. Many instruction books tell you "what," but you also need to know "how", "how much", "when" and "how often". Our program answers all of those questions, giving you the complete short game instruction book that you deserve.

We are finally giving you what has been available in every other sport for years: a clear series of steps to follow to become better. In basketball, you learn to dribble, pass, shoot, play defense, etc. through a series of progressive drills that makes playing basketball second nature. In learning to type, you follow a pattern that insures your improvement through learning the keys, then measures your progress with timed tests. Learning to swim involves a clear series of steps: floating, leg kick, arm motion and breathing.

What if we tried to skip a few steps in learning to type or swim? Would we be able to get a few tips from Typing Digest to make up for those missing habits? We all know the answer. Our habits will determine how good we are at typing. Does it take hours of practice per day to become a proficient typist? No. It takes consistently doing the right things for a reasonable period of time (a 3.5-month semester is pretty common for those learning in school).

We are asking you to commit 12 weeks to our program and follow all the all the steps we outline here. As with any other serious pursuit, you will develop habits that will become second nature to you.

You have the potential to be better than you are right now. What is a 12-week commitment when you can gain a lifetime of better golf? We just ask that you trust us. We've done the work and performed the research, and we can recall hundreds and even thousands of students who have enjoyed dramatic improvement.

Here's a quick example: When I first saw Michael he had just shot 127 in a tournament. It was a shock to his system. He knew he wasn't a great player, but he thought his game would hold up better in competition than that. Over the next several weeks he learned the principles you are going to learn in this book. He set up a practice routine similar to the platinum time plan you will learn about, and within 12 weeks his short game had improved dramatically. Within 14 months he had broken 80, and he now regularly shoots in the mid-70s.

This could be you.

"We challenge you to see what your potential is. No excuses."

I GOT A LATE START IN GOLF.

Tour players don't normally take up the game at age 19. But after five years of learning golf on my own, I had a low single-digit handicap, and a chance elective class I took in college led to the far-fetched idea of becoming a PGA Tour player (far-fetched according to my family and friends, anyway). That elective was called "Special Topics in Business Management." I needed one more elective hour and I heard it was an easy A. I was two quarters away from graduation and still didn't know what I wanted to do with my life. Our textbooks were *Think and Grow Rich* by Napolean Hill and *How to Win Friends and Influence People* by Dale Carnegie. One day, midway through the quarter, the professor came in and said something that changed my life. He asked: "If you could do anything you wanted to do and there was no limit on what you could do, what would you choose to do?" I had never thought about it that way. My passion for golf was to the point that I could be first on the tee at 7:00 am Saturday and Sunday,

My Golf Story

— Charlie King

but couldn't quite get myself out of bed for my 9:00 am classes during the week. I had attended the 1987 Masters and witnessed one of the greatest shots in golf history, the chip-in by Larry Mize on the 11th hole to beat Greg Norman in a playoff, so it seemed logical to me to answer my professor's question with: "I would win the Masters." Inspired, I went to my two-bedroom apartment and got out a notebook. I wrote down my goal to win the Masters at the top and wrote the steps it would take from A to Z. I pursued my dream as hard as I could for four years. Then, at age 28, having had very limited success, I decided it was time to move on. But, needless to say, there had been benefits to chasing my dream, even if they weren't immediately evident. I had worked with several teachers in addition to becoming one myself. My first teacher "methodized" me with a one-size fits all approach that was ridiculous, to say the least. I had teachers whose philosophies changed from week to week, and a couple who simply did not care. It was a disgrace. Their examples taught me what not to do. And I can make that knowledge work for you. I have no idea if I could have made it on Tour, but **I deserved a chance to reach my potential. And so do you.** You deserve an approach that makes sense. In the pages that follow, we'll lay out that approach, clearly and concisely, and if you follow our system for 12 weeks you will see tremendous improvement in your game in as little as 5 minutes a day. Guaranteed. Enjoy the process, and start playing the golf you have only dreamed of playing.

2

THE
RED ZONE
SKILLS TEST

WHY DON'T PEOPLE

practice their short game when they know how important it is? We think there are lots of reasons, and we understand them.

• The full swing is more exciting at first. Being able to hit a golf ball farther than Mark McGwire could hit a home run is addictive.

• You start a hole with a tee shot, and although the stats show that there are more short-game shots than tee shots, the tee shot sets the tone for the hole. You are either in great position ready to attack the hole, or you in trouble looking to salvage the hole.

• Working on the short game can seem boring compared to a solid full shot.

So how can you change your thinking? How does the short game earn its rightful spot in your practice regimen?

It's time to set aside that adrenaline rush you get from jacking a thunderous drive and focus on a

different kind of pleasure: The pleasure of saving strokes. Lower scores will be your best reward. It's time for you to take control of your game. And it starts in close. You want red numbers? Master the Red Zone.

By using Athlon's Red Zone Short Game Skills Test, you can accurately assess your Red Zone proficiency — your strengths, your weaknesses, where you need to get better. Our Red Zone scoring system allows you to evaluate your current skill level numerically, and it gives you a baseline by which you can measure your progress. Call this step the weigh-in before the diet begins. It can be painful, but it's necessary, and it's the first step in our 12-week road to improvement.

> **We want you to test and rate yourself in six categories:**
>
> **1. Wedges from 100 yards and in**
> **2. Bunker**
> **3. Pitching around the green**
> **4. Chipping**
> **5. Long putting**
> **6. Short putting**

1) Wedge Shots

For your wedge shots, place targets at distances of 20, 40, 60, 80 and 100 yards, then fire away. If you can't get your friends to serve as targets, use handy, visible objects like bag stands.

2) Bunker Shots

Gary Player used to practice his bunker shots until he holed out a certain number. If you're not at that level, simply put 10 bunker shots as close to the pin as possible to give yourself a score.

3) Pitching

In baseball, pitching is everything. It's big in golf, too. Hit 10 shots from around the green to give yourself a pitching handicap.

4) Chipping

Chipping can be your secret weapon. But first, figure out how much work you have to do. Hit 10 shots from the fringe and measure the results.

5) Long Putting

Unless you're a pro who's always firing at pins, lag putting from 20 feet and out is critically important. Hit two putts each from 20, 30, 40, 50 and 60 feet to give yourself a long putting score.

6) Short Putting

Holing those 12- to 15-footers can erase all kinds of mistakes. Grade your short putting by hitting two putts apiece from 3, 6, 9, 12 and 15 feet.

PURPOSE

To accurately evaluate your present skill level using a scoring system. This test allows you to have a measurable account of your progress.

DIRECTIONS

Using the test at the top of the following page, write in the score you have earned according to the scoring system for each Red Zone category. Then log your results on the accompanying chart to give yourself a handicap for each category. Using this systematic approach, you can create an efficient improvement plan and attack it aggressively. Then use the instruction from Rob and Charlie on the following pages to start chipping away (pun intended) at that handicap. Your scores will plummet while your confidence and efficiency from 100 yards and in will soar. Guaranteed.

The thing that really makes this test unique is that we give you a handicap in each individual category. As a golfer you understand what a 20 handicap is. With this test, you'll understand what a 20 putting handicap is, or a 30 bunker handicap. The ultimate goal? Lower your handicap, of course.

This may seem very simple, but quantifying your results is really a revolutionary concept in golf. Finding out just where you need the most improvement will result in less wasted time and more real progress.

Think about it. You may spend a lot of time on your game without seeing results on the course. You're probably beating balls on the practice tee when you should be honing your Red Zone skills. It's time you started working on the right stuff.

You might be surprised by what you discover. Many players might carry a 14 handicap, but they chip and putt more like a 30. The Athlon Red Zone skills test will reveal that and put you on the road to real improvement.

Using the following sheet, give yourself a score in each Red Zone area. Using this systematic approach and giving yourself a handicap in each area, you can create an efficient improvement plan and attack it aggressively.

SHORT GAME HANDICAPPING SYSTEM

PURPOSE: To accurately evaluate your present skill level using a scoring system. This test allows you to have a measurable account of your progress.

1) WEDGE SHOT – 10 SHOTS
(2 from: 20, 40, 60, 80, 100 yds)

where the ball lands, target can be a bag stand or range basket. You may need a partner or teacher to help you score where your ball lands.

SCORE		
	*Hit target	3pts
	0-10 feet	2pts
	10-20 feet	1pt
	20-30 feet	0pts
	Over 30 feet	-1pt

2) BUNKER SHOT – 10 SHOTS
(From 7 to 15 yards; any lie - place the ball)

SCORE		
	Holed	3pts
	0-5 feet	2pts
	5-10 feet	1pt
	10-15 feet	0pts
	Over 15 feet	-1pt

3) PITCH SHOT – 10 SHOTS
(15 yds. from edge of green, 10-15 yds. to cup, 25 to 30 yard shot total)

SCORE		
	Holed	3pts
	0-5 feet	2pts
	5-10 feet	1pt
	10-15 feet	0pts
	Over 15 feet	-1pt

4) CHIP SHOT – 10 SHOTS
(From fringe - 5 from 45 ft. and 5 from 60 ft)

SCORE		
	Holed	3pts
	0-3 feet	2pts
	3-6 feet	1pt
	6-9 feet	0pts
	Over 9 feet	-1pt

5) LONG PUTTING – 10 PUTTS
(To same hole; 2 from: 20, 30, 40, 50, 60 ft)

SCORE		
	Holed	3pts
	0-3 feet	2pts
	3-6 feet	1pt
	6-9 feet	0pts
	Over 9 feet	-1pt

6) SHORT PUTTING – 20 PUTTS
(2 putts to same hole from 3, 6, 9, 12, 15 feet L-R)
(2 putts to same hole from 3, 6, 9, 12, 15 feet R-L)

SCORE		
	Holed	2pts

TOT
SCO

Use the accompanying chart to log your scores and give yourself a Red Zone Handicap.

SHORT GAME HANDICAPPING SYSTEM

1. WEDGE	2. BUNKER	3. PITCHING	4. CHIPPING	5. LONG PUTTING	6. SHORT PUTTING	OVERALL HANDICAP
=+5	20=+5	22=+5	22=+5	24=+5	26=+5	100-106=scratch
=+3	18=+3	20=+3	20=+3	22=+3		
=scratch	16=scratch	18=scratch		20=scratch	24=+3	95-99= 2
=1	15= 1	17= 1	18=scratch	18= 2		90-94= 3
=3	14= 2	16= 2	17= 2	17= 4	20=scratch	
=4	13= 3	15= 4	16= 4	16= 6		85-89= 4
=5	12= 4	14= 5	15= 6	15= 8	18= 3	80-84= 5
=7	11= 5	13= 7	14= 8	14=10		
=9	10= 6	12= 8	13=10	13=12	16= 6	75-79= 7
=10	9= 7	11=10	12=12	12=14	14= 9	66-74= 9
=12	8= 8	10=11	11=14	11=16		55-65=12
=14	7= 9	9=13	10=16	10=18	12=12	44-54=15
=16	6=10	8=14	9=18	9=20		
=18	5=11	7=16	8=20	8=22	10=15	36-43=18
=20	4=12	6=18	7=22	7=24	8=18	29-35=21
=22	3=14	5=20	6=24	6=26		20-28=24
=24	2=16	4=22	5=26	5=28	6=21	13-19=27
=26	1=18	3=24	4=28	4=30		6-12=30
=28	0=20	2=26	3=30	3=32	4=24	
=30	-1=22	1=28	2=32	2=34	2=27	0-5=33
=32	-2=24	0=30	1=34	1=36		<0=36-39
=34	-3=26	-1=32			0=30	
=36	-4=30	-2=34				
	-5=32	-3=36				
	-6=34					
	-7=36					

WRITE IN YOUR HANDICAPS BY CATEGORY

WEDGE	BUNKER	PITCHING	CHIPPING	LONG PUTTING	SHORT PUTTING	OVERALL HANDICAP

3

THE RED ZONE CHALLENGE

JACK NICKLAUS FACED

his 40th birthday in a surprising predicament: The game's greatest player, no longer able to hit it stiff at will, needed to find himself a short game. Even after two decades of dominance and 15 major championships, the Golden Bear realized

he couldn't do it alone. He needed a little help, so he summoned an old buddy from his past named Phil Rodgers, who taught the great Nicklaus a little pendulum chip. The result? Nicklaus won two majors in 1980, and in 1986 he gave golf fans their greatest thrill with his sixth Masters title.

Our point in all this: If a 40-year-old Jack Nicklaus needed direction to re-master his short game, do you think you can do it alone, through trial and error?

It's almost impossible to stumble upon a short game that you'll be happy with. Without directions, you're doomed to wander aimlessly until frustration drives you away from the course.

Well, we've got a destination in mind — and we've also got a set of directions on how to get you there.

We have created this system because golf lacks a clearly defined roadmap to success, and you deserve to have one. You need to know the things to do daily that will have the biggest effect on your game. As you will see, we are giving three different levels of time commitment depending on how busy your life is.

All we ask is that you stick with this for 12 weeks.

> " We have created this system because golf lacks a clearly defined roadmap to success, and you deserve to have one. "

The 12-Week Challenge

So, before we get to the "How," let's quickly go over the "What." What do I need to commit to do to be a better Red Zone player?

In the chapters that follow, we'll be giving you all the information you need to improve your short game. In Chapter 12, titled 5 Minutes to Better Golf™, we give you simple daily exercises for putting what you learn into practice.

But what should you do with all this information? Here are three simple steps that answer that question.

Step 1

Decide on your level of time commitment. We recommend that you choose from one of three levels:

• **The Silver program** is a 1.5-hour commitment per week. That hour and a half includes daily drills (except for the seventh day) and one practice session per week at a short game area. This program is for the busy golfer who can squeeze one trip to the short game area per week and one and a half hours total per week into his or her schedule. The indoor 5 Minutes to Better Golf™ exercises are designed for everybody, but specifically for the golfer with limited time. If you consistently do your putting drills, posture and grip in the mirror, along with the impact exercises, you will see amazing improvement. Why? Because when you do anything consistently it becomes a habit.

• **The Gold program** is a 3-hour commitment per week. Your 5 Minutes to Better Golf™ exercises will be supplemented by two sessions at a short game area. The Gold program is for the golfer who can commit to three hours and two trips to the short game area per week. The Gold includes the same exercises as the Silver with more time and repetitions to make it second nature.

• **The Platinum program** is a 5-hour-plus commitment per week. This program is for the golfer who is looking for maximum results. If you want, you can build in fitness and strength training, tournament play and performance skills as well as your golf skills.

Step 2

Study the Essentials of the Short Game™ skills that we outline in Chapters 4 through 8. By focusing on what to do instead of what not to do, you will improve faster than if you used traditional methods.

Step 3

Go through the Commitment Process in Chapter 9 to make certain that you will follow through for the entire 12 weeks and beyond. When the "Why" is strong enough, we figure out how to do the rest. Then, follow our step-by-step instructions and have faith that this book includes the best short-game wisdom we have to offer, and that those who follow it will see measurable improvement.

Directions for the 12-Week Charts

Here, we outline the three commitment levels and the accompanying requirements. They're simple and easy to follow if you observe these recommendations:

1. The 5 Minutes to Better Golf™ in the chart refers to doing each of your most critical indoor drills six days a week.

2. When the chart refers to "Short Game area", that means that you are to pick a specific short game area and spend 30 minutes of practice time in that area.

3. For touch and feel, the more you can practice outside, the better.

4. Make an X on each day as you complete the task.

5. When you play, keep track of putts, up-and-downs from 40 yards and in, sand saves and up-and-downs from 100 yards and in.

The Athlon Red Zone Challenge
12 Week Training Schedule (Silver)

Week	M	T	W	T	F	S	S
1	minutes better golf	5 minutes to better golf	Short Game area, 5 minutes to better golf	5 minutes to better golf	5 minutes to better golf	Play Golf, 5 minutes to better golf	Off
2	minutes better golf	5 minutes to better golf	Short Game area, 5 minutes to better golf	5 minutes to better golf	5 minutes to better golf	Play Golf, 5 minutes to better golf	Off
3	minutes better golf	5 minutes to better golf	Short Game area, 5 minutes to better golf	5 minutes to better golf	5 minutes to better golf	Play Golf, 5 minutes to better golf	Off
4	minutes better golf	5 minutes to better golf	Short Game area, 5 minutes to better golf	5 minutes to better golf	5 minutes to better golf	Play Golf, 5 minutes to better golf	Off
5	minutes better golf	5 minutes to better golf	Short Game area, 5 minutes to better golf	5 minutes to better golf	5 minutes to better golf	Play Golf, 5 minutes to better golf	Off
6	minutes better golf	5 minutes to better golf	Short Game area, 5 minutes to better golf	5 minutes to better golf	5 minutes to better golf	Play Golf, 5 minutes to better golf	Off
7	minutes better golf	5 minutes to better golf	Short Game area, 5 minutes to better golf	5 minutes to better golf	5 minutes to better golf	Play Golf, 5 minutes to better golf	Off
8	minutes better golf	5 minutes to better golf	Short Game area, 5 minutes to better golf	5 minutes to better golf	5 minutes to better golf	Play Golf, 5 minutes to better golf	Off
9	minutes better golf	5 minutes to better golf	Short Game area, 5 minutes to better golf	5 minutes to better golf	5 minutes to better golf	Play Golf, 5 minutes to better golf	Off
10	minutes better golf	5 minutes to better golf	Short Game area, 5 minutes to better golf	5 minutes to better golf	5 minutes to better golf	Play Golf, 5 minutes to better golf	Off
11	minutes better golf	5 minutes to better golf	Short Game area, 5 minutes to better golf	5 minutes to better golf	5 minutes to better golf	Play Golf, 5 minutes to better golf	Off
12	minutes better golf	5 minutes to better golf	Short Game area, 5 minutes to better golf	5 minutes to better golf	5 minutes to better golf	Play Golf, 5 minutes to better golf	Off

The Athlon Red Zone Challenge
12 Week Training Schedule (Gold)

Week 1

M	T	W	T	F	S	S
5 minutes to better golf	5 minutes to better golf	Short Game area, 5 minutes to better golf	5 minutes to better golf	Short Game area, 5 minutes to better golf	Play Golf, 5 minutes to better golf	Off

Week 2

M	T	W	T	F	S	S
5 minutes to better golf	5 minutes to better golf	Short Game area, 5 minutes to better golf	5 minutes to better golf	Short Game area, 5 minutes to better golf	Play Golf, 5 minutes to better golf	Off

Week 3

M	T	W	T	F	S	S
5 minutes to better golf	5 minutes to better golf	Short Game area, 5 minutes to better golf	5 minutes to better golf	Short Game area, 5 minutes to better golf	Play Golf, 5 minutes to better golf	Off

Week 4

M	T	W	T	F	S	S
5 minutes to better golf	5 minutes to better golf	Short Game area, 5 minutes to better golf	5 minutes to better golf	Short Game area, 5 minutes to better golf	Play Golf, 5 minutes to better golf	Off

Week 5

M	T	W	T	F	S	S
5 minutes to better golf	5 minutes to better golf	Short Game area, 5 minutes to better golf	5 minutes to better golf	Short Game area, 5 minutes to better golf	Play Golf, 5 minutes to better golf	Off

Week 6

M	T	W	T	F	S	S
5 minutes to better golf	5 minutes to better golf	Short Game area, 5 minutes to better golf	5 minutes to better golf	Short Game area, 5 minutes to better golf	Play Golf, 5 minutes to better golf	Off

Week 7

M	T	W	T	F	S	S
5 minutes to better golf	5 minutes to better golf	Short Game area, 5 minutes to better golf	5 minutes to better golf	Short Game area, 5 minutes to better golf	Play Golf, 5 minutes to better golf	Off

Week 8

M	T	W	T	F	S	S
5 minutes to better golf	5 minutes to better golf	Short Game area, 5 minutes to better golf	5 minutes to better golf	Short Game area, 5 minutes to better golf	Play Golf, 5 minutes to better golf	Off

Week 9

M	T	W	T	F	S	S
5 minutes to better golf	5 minutes to better golf	Short Game area, 5 minutes to better golf	5 minutes to better golf	Short Game area, 5 minutes to better golf	Play Golf, 5 minutes to better golf	Off

Week 10

M	T	W	T	F	S	S
5 minutes to better golf	5 minutes to better golf	Short Game area, 5 minutes to better golf	5 minutes to better golf	Short Game area, 5 minutes to better golf	Play Golf, 5 minutes to better golf	Off

Week 11

M	T	W	T	F	S	S
5 minutes to better golf	5 minutes to better golf	Short Game area, 5 minutes to better golf	5 minutes to better golf	Short Game area, 5 minutes to better golf	Play Golf, 5 minutes to better golf	Off

Week 12

M	T	W	T	F	S	S
5 minutes to better golf	5 minutes to better golf	Short Game area, 5 minutes to better golf	5 minutes to better golf	Short Game area, 5 minutes to better golf	Play Golf, 5 minutes to better golf	Off

The Athlon Red Zone Challenge
12 Week Training Schedule (Platinum)

	T	W	T	F	S	S
rt Game, 5 minutes etter golf	5 minutes to better golf	Short Game area, 5 minutes to better golf	5 minutes to better golf	Short Game area, 5 minutes to better golf	Play Golf, 5 minutes to better golf	Off
rt Game, 5 minutes etter golf	5 minutes to better golf	Short Game area, 5 minutes to better golf	5 minutes to better golf	Short Game area, 5 minutes to better golf	Play Golf, 5 minutes to better golf	Off
rt Game, 5 minutes etter golf	5 minutes to better golf	Short Game area, 5 minutes to better golf	5 minutes to better golf	Short Game area, 5 minutes to better golf	Play Golf, 5 minutes to better golf	Off
rt Game, 5 minutes etter golf	5 minutes to better golf	Short Game area, 5 minutes to better golf	5 minutes to better golf	Short Game area, 5 minutes to better golf	Play Golf, 5 minutes to better golf	Off
rt Game, 5 minutes etter golf	5 minutes to better golf	Short Game area, 5 minutes to better golf	5 minutes to better golf	Short Game area, 5 minutes to better golf	Play Golf, 5 minutes to better golf	Off
rt Game, 5 minutes etter golf	5 minutes to better golf	Short Game area, 5 minutes to better golf	5 minutes to better golf	Short Game area, 5 minutes to better golf	Play Golf, 5 minutes to better golf	Off
rt Game, 5 minutes etter golf	5 minutes to better golf	Short Game area, 5 minutes to better golf	5 minutes to better golf	Short Game area, 5 minutes to better golf	Play Golf, 5 minutes to better golf	Off
rt Game, 5 minutes etter golf	5 minutes to better golf	Short Game area, 5 minutes to better golf	5 minutes to better golf	Short Game area, 5 minutes to better golf	Play Golf, 5 minutes to better golf	Off
rt Game, 5 minutes etter golf	5 minutes to better golf	Short Game area, 5 minutes to better golf	5 minutes to better golf	Short Game area, 5 minutes to better golf	Play Golf, 5 minutes to better golf	Off
rt Game, 5 minutes etter golf	5 minutes to better golf	Short Game area, 5 minutes to better golf	5 minutes to better golf	Short Game area, 5 minutes to better golf	Play Golf, 5 minutes to better golf	Off
rt Game, 5 minutes etter golf	5 minutes to better golf	Short Game area, 5 minutes to better golf	5 minutes to better golf	Short Game area, 5 minutes to better golf	Play Golf, 5 minutes to better golf	Off
rt Game, 5 minutes etter golf	5 minutes to better golf	Short Game area, 5 minutes to better golf	5 minutes to better golf	Short Game area, 5 minutes to better golf	Play Golf, 5 minutes to better golf	Off

The Athlon Red Zone Challenge
Customized Player Form

Fill out the following to create a customized daily plan and then follow your 12-week calendar.
Pick 2 or 3 drills for each short game category (read chapters 4-8 or refer to the 5 Minutes to Better Golf Drills in Chapter 12):

1) Short Putting
a. _____
b. _____
c. _____

2) Long Putting
a. _____
b. _____
c. _____

3) Chipping
a. _____
b. _____
c. _____

4) Pitching
a. _____
b. _____
c. _____

5) Distance Wedges
a. _____
b. _____
c. _____

6) Bunker Play
a. _____
b. _____
c. _____

The 5 Minutes to Better Golf™ Exercises you pick and record in the form above should be practiced 6 days a week during your 12-week Challenge. By practicing these things consistently for short periods of time you will see improvement and have a plan that you can stick with.

We recommend you get a 9-foot putting mat for the 5 Minutes to Better Golf™ putting drills you can do at home. You need to find a mirror or reflective surface so you can master the impact position and swing plane as well as some of the specific body movements in the pitch shot and bunker shot. We will have a list of recommended training aids in the appendix.

A 12 Week Example
Eight easy steps to better golf

1) Read this book through once to get the big picture.

2) Take the Red Zone test and convert it to a Red Zone handicap. You can do this yourself or with the help of a PGA Professional.

3) Read chapters 4-8 again and look at the concepts for each part. Then look at the drills that transform these areas into strengths instead of weaknesses. Set some handicap goals for each category.

4) Fill in the two or three blanks under each category on the customized player form with the drills you picked out from the chapters and from the chapter on 5 Minutes to Better Golf™.

5) Pick a time commitment — Silver, Gold or Platinum — and stick with that training schedule for the next 12 weeks.

6) Test yourself in individual categories randomly to see how you are progressing before you take the test again at the end of the 12 weeks.

7) Take the test again at the end of the 12 weeks, see how close it came to the goals you set at the beginning and celebrate.

8) Go to athlonsports.com to enter the national contest.

THE ESSENTIALS OF A GREAT SHORT GAME™

NOW IT IS TIME FOR THE

details. In the next several chapters we will lay out the fundamentals of each short game shot and the drills that give you the feel of how to do each one. Our goal in this is not to be more clever than the other short game books in the past. Our goal is to create for you an overall understanding and plan that will lead to your improvement.

You don't just need the fundamentals. And a plan of daily exercises won't do much good without the essential principles. We want to give you the ESSENTIALS of the Short Game.

As we said earlier, we've heard students say, "I don't care about my short game until I can get on or near the green. I want you to help me hit it better." We understand that way of thinking.

But we are going to help your whole game. Starting with the putter and working our way out, we'll be giving you Essentials that will create improvement all the way up to your driver. The Essentials of putting transfer to better chipping, which transfers to better pitching and so on. Small swings and slower swings provide the best way to learn. That's why working on your short game has such a great overall effect.

At some point you will reach that level where you realize it is your short game holding your game back, and when you do, these are the Essentials that will help your game.

The first step in the learning process is eliminating the misconceptions that are hurting your game. To prepare you for our program of improvement, we want to get these out on the table and then eliminate them.

Then, when you get to Chapter 4 and start getting the right ideas for Red Zone improvement, you'll see that we've cut out the fluff and filler to give you Golf's Greatest Hits.

Updating Your Software
Golf's Fallacies, Misconceptions and Deadly Instincts

Just like having outdated software or a virus in your computer, misconceptions create problems with your brain's circuitry. We need to get rid of them. Not all of these are Red Zone-specific, but they need to be dealt with before serious improvement can become a reality.

Golf's Major Misconceptions
"You're lifting your head" or "You looked up"

This is the faulty belief that hitting a golf shot is simply hand-eye coordination. It is believed that if you don't make good contact, it is because you took your eye off the ball. Our comeback to this faulty idea is that staring at piano keys is not going to make you a good piano player. There are a lot of other elements that go into playing a piano other than watching the keys. This concept can also be applied to golf. "Seeing" the golf ball is only a small part of the entire swing. The hands, arms, wrists, and shoulders all must be trained to bottom out the club in the right place to produce solid contact.

Taking the club "straight back and straight through" will create straight shots

On the surface, this seems logical, but because we stand to the side, and the club is shaped the way it is, the shape of the swing is not straight back and straight through, but a circle tilted over, an arc. This concept relates to the master task of path/face combination, which you will read about in a following section.

"Keep the left arm straight"

There is a glimmer of truth in this because we are trying to maintain width in our golf swing; unfortunately, the concept has led to tension-filled golf swings.

"Keep the head still"

This directive in conjunction with "Keep the left arm straight" leads to a reverse pivot - a player's weight is on the front foot during the backswing and transferred to the back foot on the forwardswing.

"Effort/Muscle/Strength = Power"

You want effortless club head speed. Swinging harder and being stronger will not necessarily create greater distance in your golf swing. The correct formula is clubhead speed + solid contact = distance.

"Don't leave this one short" or "Make sure you don't kill it"

Misconceptions in putting are fewer and have more to do with our fears. Putting is the simplest act in golf, but not the simplest to master. Just look at the effect putting poorly has on tour players long-term. Losing touch on the greens has driven many great players to unique grips and long putters. Chapter 4 will give you a game plan to make this a strong part of your game.

Golf's 3 Deadly Instincts ...

So much of golf is contrary to what our instincts tell us. So, to get us started, let's look at what golfers instinctively want to do — but shouldn't do — when we swing a golf club. I know the word "deadly" sounds a little harsh, but so are chunking a ball into the water and skulling it across the green.

If a person walks onto a tee to hit a golf ball without any previous instruction, there are three deadly instincts that invariably take over. Left uncorrected, they create some bad habits. But once you identify and counteract these instincts, you will see vast improvement.

The deadly instincts: Scoop It, Steer It, Kill It

Here they are in order of "deadliness":

1) Golfers try to "lift" the ball into the air

Rather than "striking" the ball, golfers will try to "scoop" the ball into the air. With a scooping motion, the weight stays back, and the player hits on top of the ball or too far behind the ball. To make matters worse, the golfer is then told - incorrectly - that he lifted his head. With a bad diagnosis, you can't get better.

2) Golfers try to steer or guide the ball towards the target

Taking the club straight through to the target seems logical, but because we stand to the side, and the club is shaped the way it is, the shape of the swing is not straight back and straight through, but a tilted circle. The more you steer to hit it straight, the more crooked the ball goes.

3) Golfers try to kill the ball

When the instinct to "kill" takes over, bad things happen. Swinging with rhythm and creating effortless clubhead speed is the better way to achieve distance than exerting a lot of energy, but it certainly doesn't seem correct.

Now, let's replace these misconceptions and deadly instincts with the correct concepts, and get started on lowering your score.

4

> " There is no similarity between golf and putting; they are two different games — one played in the air, the other on the ground.
>
> Ben Hogan "

PUTTING

HOW IMPORTANT IS PUTTING?

Dumb question, right? Putting is so important that it has been described as a "game within the game." Another way to put it: The object of the game is to put the ball in the hole in the least number of strokes. Finding the hole is accomplished over 96% of the time with the putter. In other words — you complete your ultimate objective with the putter in your hands. It doesn't get much more important than that.

To putt well, you must accomplish two simple tasks. First of all, roll the ball well. Secondly, roll it on line. This seems obvious, but there are some psychological and visual barriers to doing these two things.

Barriers to Good Putting

1) The size of the hole

-The small diameter of the hole (4.25 inches) gives the golfer the feeling of having to be perfect.

2) Standing sideways causes a visual distortion

-When reading the putt from directly behind the hole you can see the line as it is. When you stand sideways as you address the ball, you are seeing a distorted image that may be fooling you.

3) Poor practice habits

- Haphazard practice leads to less than stellar results. By practicing in a way that insures success, you develop good habits and your confidence grows.

4) Fear

-Fear, anxiety and nerves — a time-tested recipe for poor performances on the greens.

Following our plan over a 12-week period is going to eliminate these barriers and let you focus on the Essentials of Putting™ outlined here.

Roll the Ball Well

Let's define this term a little more clearly: Rolling the ball well happens when the putter is swung smoothly, the ball is hit solidly and the speed takes the ball into or near the hole. Most of us have learned to putt with our only guide being the motivation and pressure of trying to make it. We need to shift the focus to a good stroke with good speed control.

Putting is perhaps more feel-oriented than anything else in golf, but there are some real-world techniques that you can use to take putting out of the realm of pure guesswork. Repeat these drills, and long putting will become almost as natural as walking.

Drills

1) Pendulum Drill — Swing the putter back and forth with a 'tick, tock' beat. Find a 20- or 30-foot putt and count an even 'tick, tock' to yourself as you putt the ball. Watch the ball roll all the way and notice if you hit it too hard, too easy or just right.

Let the putter swing freely between your thumb and forefinger to get a feel for the natural tick, tock rhythm.

Do this for at least five minutes to keep your focus on the pendulum feel. Over a period of 12 weeks this will become second nature.

2) Look at the Hole Drill — One of our favorites. This drill is simple. Instead of looking at the ball as you putt, look at the hole. Free-throw shooters don't focus on the ball; they look at the hoop. Like basketball and other sports where you get a good sense of the target by looking at it, the same thing happens in your putting. After the first few awkward putts, most golfers notice they develop an uncanny sense of speed and direction. Golfers have an innate sense of touch; they simply need something to draw it out of them. This drill does it.

3) Right Hand Only Drill — When putting with one hand, golfers naturally swing the putter and don't guide the ball. This leads to a sense of truly rolling the ball and not over-controlling and guiding it.

4) The "Don't Look" Drill — This drill forces you to take

the feel of the other drills and put it to the test. Find a spot 30 to 40 feet from the cup and putt the ball toward the hole. Before you look up, you must guess how far the ball is from the hole in terms of distance and direction. If you are correct or close, you have drawn out your feel of how far to hit the ball. This is sometimes referred to as the 'mind's eye.' You will find that this drill

4

Before you look up, try to picture how close to the hole the ball is. This will help your feel immeasurably.

yourself to keep your head still. Position yourself so that the shadow of your head falls over some point of reference, like the hole. Then watch your shadow while you make some practice strokes. If your head moves during your stroke, it will be obvious to you (photos C and D). Practice your putting stroke while keeping your head's shadow positioned over the reference point, and you'll learn to putt with your head still (photos A and B). Simple but effective.

Do these drills as we prescribe in the Challenge and you will watch your ability to roll the ball get noticeably better by test time and, most importantly, on the golf course.

will help you get better and better at feeling how far to hit the ball.

5) The Shadow Knows — Moving your head while putting can lead to a variety of problems, but there's a simple way to train

5

Yes: Your head's shadow stays over the hole

No: If your head doesn't remain still, your shadow will let you know

A B

C D

Roll the Ball On-Line

This is the more detailed part of putting, and it's received most of the ink — how to grip, stand, line up, etc. These things are also essential, but having a fundamentally sound stroke and not knowing how to 'roll' the ball is a big mistake. The following Essentials will help us in our quest to start more putts on line. Match these essentials with the 'feel' you learned in the previous section, and you'll be draining 20-footers.

Left: Reverse Overlap Grip. Right: Left Hand Low Grip

Putting Essentials™

1) Grip and Setup

The Essential in gripping the putter is to create a proactive relationship between your hands and the putter face. Many different grips have worked over the years, but there is one Essential that these successful grips have all had in common: They all square the clubface at contact. Here, we show you the reverse overlap grip, which is the most common, as well as the left-hand low grip.

Our Setup Essential is designed to create a consistent arc and path for the putter.

1) Bend over from the hips
2) Eyes slightly inside the target line and behind the ball
3) Hands and arms hang right below the shoulders
4) Shoulders and forearms are parallel to the target
5) Forearms are in line with the shaft
6) Ball position in front of your dominant eye
7) Maintain grip pressure

2) Face Control

The face must be pointed at the intended target to get the ball to go there. We know that statement seems obvious, but it is surprising how many people don't play or practice as if the face angle is the most important factor. In our drills section you'll find the best and most effective drills for making this into a strength.

3) Speed Control

This is what we talked about earlier. Assuming reasonable path, face and centered hits, you need to hit a putt and then adjust by feel. Our goal is to "unlock" your feel with a series of drills. Don't change mechanics or agonize over it. Trying to be perfect on every putt leads to tightness and is a roadblock to your feel. Let the brain feel a long putt and a short putt, and it will calculate the middle between the two. It becomes more like tossing a ball.

4) Hitting the ball on a consistent spot on the clubface

It is important to hit the ball on the same spot on the putter every time so you know how the ball will react off the putter. Notice that we said the "same" spot, not necessarily the "sweet" spot. We recommend the sweet spot, but we also understand why Isao Aoki is a good putter. His ball reacts the same way each time even though he is hitting the ball with the heel of the putter.

5) Aim

Aligning in putting is inherently more difficult because we have to stand sideways. This creates a distorted image as we look at our target. To become proficient at lining up, we suggest you use training aids such as the chalk line, the stakes and string and the credit card drill.

6) Path

Your putter has at least a 10-degree angle by the rules of golf. This angle must be taken into account when swinging the putter most efficiently. On short putts, there may be an appearance of straight back and straight through. There is still an ever-so-tiny arc. Later in the chapter we list the best drills and training aids to perfect your path.

7) Swing the club

The to-and-fro motion that comprises a swing is necessary even in a small putting stroke. The rhythm and flow of a swing breeds consistency in your putting. The Pendulum Drill from earlier in the chapter is designed to help you develop this Essential.

• As we turn to the drills, you'll notice that we've referenced the applicable putting essentials with each drill. Use these notations to maximize your practice time.

Get the Ball On-line:

Drills

1) Putting String

(Essentials 2, 5, 6)

This is one of our favorites. You can work on improving straight putts and breaking putts. This aid helps your path, face control and a pattern of success for confidence. Affix a length of string to two pencils, then stick the pencils in the ground so that the string is taut. Place the ball underneath the string, then use the string as your guide.

2) Your Credit Card Can Make You Money

(Essentials 2, 5, 6)

A: Find yourself a straight-on 8-foot putt. Once you think you've lined up correctly, have your buddy replace the ball with a credit card. The card will tell you the exact direction your putter face is pointing. **B/C**: Place the ball on top of the card, and putt.

2) Your Credit Card Can Make You Money — Credit cards tend to get us in trouble financially, but we've found a way to get your credit card to make money for you.

The putter face must be pointed at the intended target to get the ball to go there, as obvious as that may seem. Lining up perfectly is difficult when you're standing sideways, as we do in putting, but there's a solution.

Find a straight putt from about 8 feet, and line up to the heart of the hole. When you think you are lined up correctly, move the ball away, pull out your credit card and align the edge of the putter with the edge of the card (It's better if you have a partner to line the card up for you).

Now, stand back and look at where the card is pointed. This will tell you if you're lined up correctly. If your alignment is good, keep doing what you are doing. If your alignment is poor, use the credit card as an alignment aid by lining it up to your intended target; then place a ball on the card and putt off the top of it.

When you look toward the hole, you will get progressively better by seeing what straight really looks like. Then when you take the card away you will be able to line the putter up to the hole and take it there when you putt.

This simple drill will allow you to consistently control your face angle when putting and make those money putts. Use that credit card correctly, and people will start owing you money.

3) The Arc Board

(Essentials 5, 6)
By allowing the putter to follow the slightly tilted board, you create the feel for a perfect path.

4) Putting Mat

(All Essentials)

Watching the ball go in and creating a pattern of success is the key to the putting mat. Many of these drills in this section should be adapted to the mat.

5) Rubber Band Drill

(Essential 4)
Put a rubber band on either side of the sweet spot of your putter. Hit the sweet spot and there is no problem. Hit the rubber band and the ball will go sideways.

6) Putting Laser

(Essentials 2, 6)

With this revolutionary aid, you can visually train yourself to correct your putting and shave strokes off your game. This putter allows you to feel for the first time what a correct, consistent putter alignment and stroke feels like.

By accurately positioning two laser beams — one allowing you to monitor the face alignment, and the other, the path of your stroke — you can now see what perfect feels like.

My putter allows you to:

• Practice your putting with perfect alignment

• Monitor the path of your stroke backwards and forwards

• Monitor the putter face during the stroke

• Find out what a correct alignment and putter path and face feel like

• See any deviation or manipulation of the path and face throughout the stroke

• Repeat this process to exact terms

• Establish a muscle memory repeating stroke through daily practice

Available with green laser beams (my patented SOCRATES Putting Aide) or red laser beams (the PLATO Putting Aide — perfect for the Red Zone). To order, visit robakinsgolf.com.

- Rob Akins

7) Metronome

(Essentials 3, 7)

Listening to and emulating the steady beat of a metronome will help you develop the tick-tock rhythm we talked about earlier.

8) Mirror Drill

(Essentials 1, 6)
Make putting strokes while looking in a mirror.
You will see the arc and make it a habit.

9) Metal Ruler Drill

(Essentials 2, 5, 6)

This is a great alignment drill. Place a metal ruler on the ground pointing to the hole on what you think is the proper line. Then place the ball at the end of the ruler and putt. The results will reveal any alignment flaws.

1) Putt to a Tee on the green or a Dime on a Putting Mat

By selecting a target that's even smaller than the hole, you learn superior focus and precision on the greens. This one is Rob Akins' personal favorite.

2) Indifference Drill — Putt 5 balls into the hole from one foot, 4 from two feet, 3 from three feet, 2 from four feet and 1 from five feet. Then go in reverse, 1 from five, etc. If you can make it from start to finish without missing, you are done. Many golfers get ahead of themselves and miss a short one. It forces you to stay focused.

3) Around the Horn — This drill was designed by Dr. Rick Jensen. Find a hole that has enough break from the side angles that you have to play the ball outside the hole. Putt from three feet at four spots equidistant around the hole, then four feet at all four spots, then five feet at all four spots. Starting at three feet, make three putts in a row and then move to the next spot. As long as you don't miss, you keep moving to the next spot. If you miss, you must start the goal of making three in a row again. You keep track of your total number of misses. When you have finished from the last five-foot spot, you have your total number of misses. The Tour norm for the best putters is two or three total misses.

4) Red Zone Putting Tests — Periodically take this portion of the Red Zone skills test to see how you are progressing.

(RED ZONE TIP) SPEED VS. LINE

They're the two most important elements of putting, but they often seem to conflict with one another as an amateur approaches his putt. On the longer putts, amateurs often worry too much about the line and totally misjudge the speed, leaving themselves with a tough second putt. Then, when they stand over that second putt, they often worry so much about the speed that they forget to judge the line properly. The result? Way too many three-putts. Sound familiar?

I want you to reverse your thinking as you stand over your putts. On the longer putts, especially those of 15 feet or more, the speed is much more important than the line. Instead of worrying so much about the line, I want you to envision a path to the hole that's 8-10 inches wide, and to play maximum break. The speed is the critical thing on those long lag putts. This approach will leave you with much more makeable second putts and curtail those dreaded three-putts.

When you get close, reverse that thinking. The shorter the putt, the less you focus on the speed. Here's where you get precise with the line. Pick a small speck where the ball will drop into the hole. You might even want to take some of the break out of the equation on the short putts.

Putting is a mental exercise. If you train your mind to approach it properly, you'll be amazed at the results.

Remember. . .

• On the long putts, envision a wider path to the hole, play maximum break and focus on the speed.

• On the short putts, concern yourself less with the speed and focus on the line, maybe even taking out some of the break.

Reading the Greens

The main thing with reading the greens is experience. The more you putt and observe, the better you will become at reading greens.

1) Always watch the ball roll until it stops. Many amateur golfers make the mistake of not watching the ball all the way until it stops. The more information you brain has, the better it can calculate for the future.

2) Look at the putt from below the hole to get a better read. If all you do is look at the putt from behind the ball, you are missing some vital information. Looking from all around is typically unnecessary and hurts speed of play, but looking from below the hole is must.

3) Visualize. To be able to see the putt in your mind before you actually putt it is very important. Putt in the morning with dew on the greens so you can see the line the putt took. Putt while looking at the hole, as we advised earlier, to see the putt roll toward the hole and how it moves.

These are a few key ideas that help you read the greens. This will become a more important topic as your stroke develops. For more detailed information on green reading, go to **www.athlonsports.com** and look for the special report titled "Advanced Techniques for Reading the Greens."

"How" to Practice Putting

1. After reading the chapter, pick at least two drills to consistently do indoors and two or more to focus on outdoors.

2. The indoor drills are what we call 5 Minutes to Better Golf™ exercises. Spend 5 minutes or more doing these six days a week during your Challenge.

3. The outdoor drills will be practiced a little longer depending on which time commitment you choose.

4. Do the individual test from time to time to challenge yourself and check your progress.

Recommended Drills Prioritized for:

Silver Program
Roll the Ball
1. Look at the Hole
2. Pendulum Drill

Get the Ball On-Line
1. Putting String
2. Credit Card Drill

Training Aids
1. Putting Mat
2. Putting Laser
3. Arc Board

Gold Program (All of the above plus)
1. Right Hand Only

1. Metal Ruler
2. Metronome
3. Rubber Band Drill
4. Mirror Drill

Platinum Program (all of the above plus)
1. Don't Look Drill

1. All the Challenge Drills

RED ZONE SUCCESS STORIES

Michael Merrill

MICHAEL NEVER THOUGHT HE would become a Golf Professional nor did he really know the difference between a 3 iron or a 7 iron when he graduated from Gettysburg College and went to work in Boston for a career wearing a suit and tie. He was introduced to the game by playing occasionally with friends here and there and was quickly drawn to the challenge of shooting low scores and the effortless look of hitting a ball 300 yards. The other reason golf was a lure for him was the emotional letdown of not competing athletically anymore after growing up with thoughts of becoming a major leaguer and playing just about every other sport there is — except golf.

He decided to abandon whatever it was he thought he wanted to be, and through John Ronis, went to work at the Wayland Golf Shop in Newton, Mass. as a sales person. Initially the expeence was similar to being dropped off in the middle of China, but e began to quickly catch on to the lingo and verbiage he needed to ecome a factor in the shop. He could not get enough golf, and he vould play almost daily that initial summer. The Wayland golf ourse was a short drive away, and he would put the first ball in the ir everyday and then get back to the golf shop by 9:00am. His aver-ge score was around 100 with an occasional high 90s round. At this tage he had had a couple of lessons from John, and his mind was nade up that his future lay in the game of golf.

That fall he arrived in Casselberry, FL for his first semester at The Golf Academy of the South to begin a 16-month golf management rogram. "My friends and family thought I had gone off the deep nd when informed of my plans, except for my mother — I could e a bank robber and she would think I should go for it." On the irst day he was informed he would play in his first tournament that

Tournament. "I followed this plan closely and with a lot of dedica-tion and energy. I have had my share of big numbers since then but I went on to become a PGA member and a Head Golf Professional.

"The message was clear and simple from Charlie that the golf swing is like any other motor skill — it is a process, not a secret. The short game was the focus of my efforts early on, and it was clearly stated by Charlie that the foundation must begin here in order for the development of my full swing to succeed properly. The plan also had to be measured and evaluated for it to be effective. Charlie's short game skills test was an essential part of my success, not only for the results but also for training to be able to execute under pressure. My overall score initially on the golf course did not come down rapidly, but I started to take solace in the fact that my testing numbers were improving. I give this test to my students at The Nantucket Golf School and it makes a substantial impact on each player to show the

His average score was around 100 with an occasional round in the high 90s. At this stage he had had a couple of lessons from John, and his mind was made up that his future lay in the game of golf.

Monday morning — 9:00 shotgun start. "I had never competed in shotgun tournament but had some experience with a shotgun unting rabbits in Vermont," Michael laughed.

Monday arrived and he reported to he starting hole with the other 100 or so students who were at various levels in their training. "My turn arrived to hit the first tee shot and the feeling in my stom-ch was one I had never experienced before in sports. Little did I know hat would be the first of 125 attempts I would make at the ball. I valked off the golf course that day feeling about as down and out as ever been in my life. Looking back on it now the next thing that happened to me that was the greatest part of this story — I met Charlie King."

"Well, Michael, we have our work cut out for us, but it can be done," Charlie said as he mapped out the plan for Michael's mprovement.

"Charlie was a teacher at The Golf Academy South and is to this lay one of the best communicators I have met in my life," Michael said.

They structured the plan, and the map that Michael followed led o his shooting a 75 only eight months later at a Monday

importance of the short game in the achieving the number one goal of all golfers-shoot lower scores. The relationship between the short game and the development of the full swing increases the value of this process of golf instruction. The 'two for one' benefit gained from a focused training program incorporating the short game leads to increased skill levels for all golfers — most important for new play-ers the game."

Michael has been teaching golf now for almost ten years. "I base my success in golf instruction on this process that Charlie instilled in me early on. Looking back now I am one of the lucky people who take up the game of golf by starting with a teacher who is passion-ate and dedicated to reaching goals. I know the process Charlie and Rob have developed works based not only on my results but on the results of students. I continue to work on my golf game with Charlie and now have the opportunity to teach along with him for various programs. He is one of the few people I have met in this game who has one focus — getting people better at golf."

5

CHIPPING

WHEN I WAS IN MY TEENS

I had the opportunity to play and practice with Randy Simmons. You may not have heard of Randy, but he played at the University of Texas during the era of Tom Kite and Ben Crenshaw. Randy was a tremendous ball-striker who insisted that we hit a bag of 150 balls with each club in the bag – 75 for him and 75 for me, with every single club. I made it pretty good through the short irons and mid-irons, but I was totally out of gas by the time we went through the long irons and the woods. I hadn't learned yet how to practice effortlessly – but that's a lesson for another time.

Then we would turn our attention to the short game and practice that just as hard. I'd say to Randy, "You hit the ball so well, why do you want to practice your chipping?" His reply: "Because I can be more aggressive when I know I can get up and down." We would start chipping, and many times Randy said to me, "When you're a good chipper, chipping gives you par for a partner." I've never heard it said better. If you can hit it near the green and are a good chipper, you can make a bunch of pars. In this chapter, Charlie and I want to give you par for a partner.

— Rob Akins

We've all admired great players like Raymond Floyd and Jose Maria Olazabal, who chip the ball so well they seem to chip in more often than they make a long putt. Emulating them is easier than you think. As with putting, once you have mastered the technique, it is the feel that will lead to great chipping. And the technique is relatively simple and straightforward, as Floyd and Olazabal will attest.

> " When you're a good chipper, chipping gives you par for a partner. "

Chipping Essentials™

The majority of golfers try to lift the ball into the air with a scooping motion. The result: The weight is on the back foot and the wrists are bending upward. We will show you how to bottom the club out and use a striking motion with an arc very similar to your putting stroke. We want you to hit the center of the loft of your club to get the ball into the air. We don't want you giving in to the scoop motion and trying to lift the ball into the air.

The great thing about chipping is this: Learning to hit a chip shot correctly leads to better ballstriking throughout the rest of your game.

Many players will break their wrist at the last second, which will result in that scooping motion and inconsistency with their chip shots. Two antidotes to scooping: Keep your hands ahead of the ball; and slightly de-loft the club. This motion will actually make getting the ball up in the air easier. You will finally be using the loft of the club correctly.

We teach the basics when it comes to chipping. When we see chipping instruction that is gimmicky, that's a sign that the teacher is in effect throwing up his hands and saying, "You can't get any better doing it the right way."

Well, we have too much respect for you to give up on you. We're assuming in this chapter that you can get better, and that you can do it the right way.

With that in mind, the keys to effective chipping are:

1) Have 70% or 80% of your weight on the left side of your body at address and keep it there throughout the swing.

2) Have the ball positioned middle to slightly back in your stance.

3) Hands slightly forward. The angle you set at address needs to reappear at impact.

4) Make a small arc with the club back and through.

5) Maintain consistent grip pressure throughout the stroke.

Oftentimes players will concentrate so much on keeping their head down, they will end up doing so too long, which restricts their body movement and encourages a scooping motion. We want you to arc up after you hit the ball, not flip the wrists up. A perfect arc both back and through is one of the secrets to great chipping.

Distance Control

Distance control and touch start with solid contact. Once you can consistently make solid contact on your chips, then you can begin to make better shots.

We recommend that you become the master of two clubs for your distance control in chipping. Use the sand wedge or pitching wedge for the short and medium chips; the 7- or 8-iron for the medium or long running chips. It is important to notice how far these clubs carry in the air and how much roll they get.

(RED ZONE TIP) **SOLID CONTACT**
Forget the one-foot putt for a second as the simplest shot in golf. Discounting the putter, the greenside chip shot is the simplest motion in golf. It doesn't take a lot of moving parts, and the swing is short. Simplest doesn't mean it's the easiest. You may be having trouble with this shot, as a lot of golfers do. I'm going to make it simpler.

The chip is defined as a low, running shot where a pitch is defined by more air time. The chip is the introduction to hitting a lofted iron. The manufacturer gave you a club that gets the ball airborne by the way it is designed as long as you hit the ball solidly. So that becomes our first goal in chipping: hit it solidly. With that in mind we are going to get the arc of our swing to hit on or past the spot where the ball sits.

All the essentials of chipping make sense if you keep hitting the ball solidly in mind. The weight should be leaning toward the left foot, the hands are slightly forward, and the ball is just back of the middle. These setup factors all encourage a solid shot. I keep mentioning solid because that is a must before you can have distance control.

In the swing, let the club make an arc going back. Don't keep the club too low or pick it up too sharply. On the forward swing, you want to avoid the most common fault in golf: the "scoop." Make sure to bump the ball with the hands leaning slightly forward.

ROB'S RULES FOR CONSISTENT CHIPPING

1) Land it on the green.
2) Land it as close to you as possible.
3) Land it on a flat spot.

Drills for Solid Contact

1) Line Drill

Brush the Grass

Take the tip of the club head and draw a line in the grass, or use tees to show the line where the ball will be. If you prefer, you can paint a line on the ground.

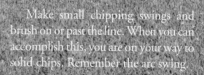

Make small chipping swings and brush on or past the line. When you can accomplish this, you are on your way to solid chips. Remember the arc swing.

Take the club you are chipping with, then take another club out of your bag and turn it over and hold the two clubs so the upside down club sticks out beside your left hip. When you chip the ball the goal is for the upside down club not to hit you in the side. If you scoop and the club hits you, that is your "punishment."

2) The Punisher Club

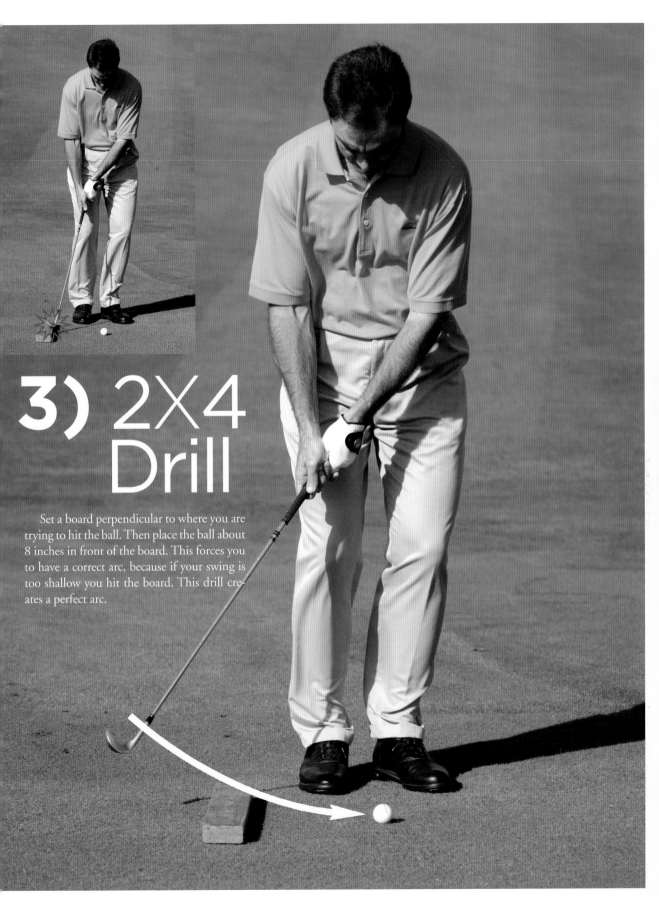

3) 2X4 Drill

Set a board perpendicular to where you are trying to hit the ball. Then place the ball about 8 inches in front of the board. This forces you to have a correct arc, because if your swing is too shallow you hit the board. This drill creates a perfect arc.

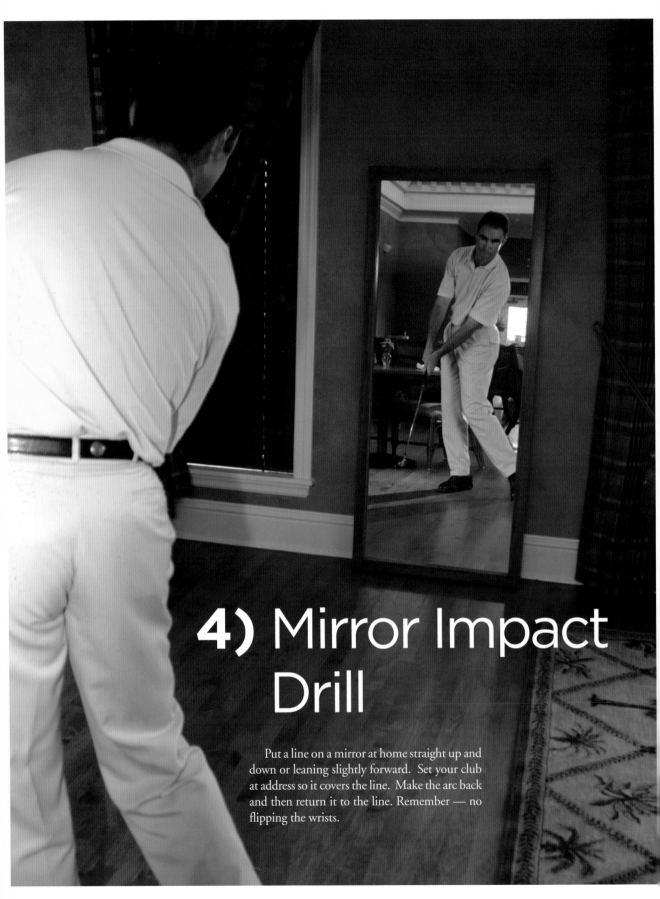

4) Mirror Impact Drill

Put a line on a mirror at home straight up and down or leaning slightly forward. Set your club at address so it covers the line. Make the arc back and then return it to the line. Remember — no flipping the wrists.

5) Look at Arms

Look at your arms and hands instead of the ball as you hit a few shots. This allows you to see if your wrist breaks down.

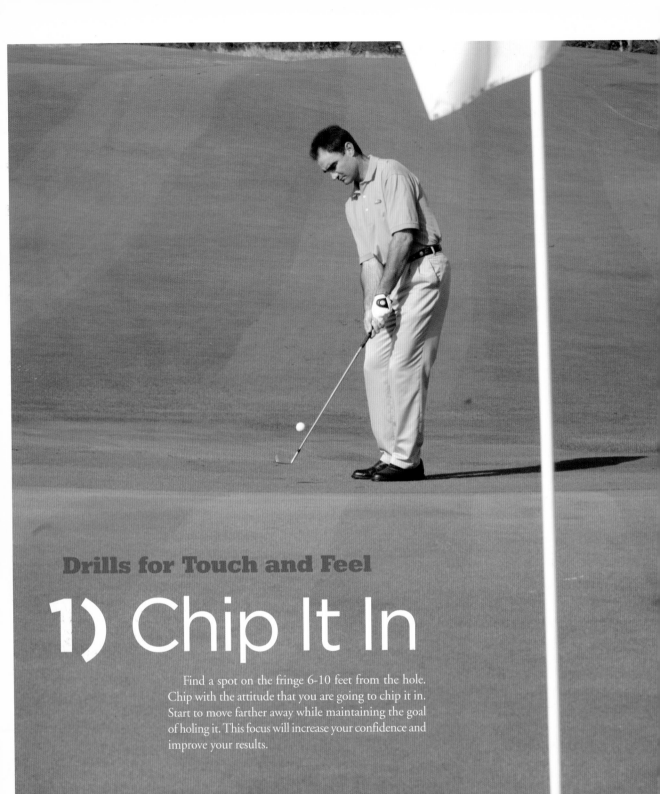

Drills for Touch and Feel

1) Chip It In

Find a spot on the fringe 6-10 feet from the hole.
Chip with the attitude that you are going to chip it in.
Start to move farther away while maintaining the goal
of holing it. This focus will increase your confidence and
improve your results.

2) Ping Pong Ball

You can use this drill inside. Hit chip shots with a ping pong ball. Notice how hitting slightly down makes the ball go up and puts some spin on the ball. Be creative and take what you learn to the real ball. I have all my juniors and many of my adult players use this drill indoors. This drill teaches my players touch, the effects of spin and imagination. It also helps you develop your intuition when chipping — that's critically important. I used to chip ping pong balls onto my dining room table at home and try to get them to stay there. It's a fun, competitive little game to play with a partner, and one that really helps you learn to shape your shots. And while you've got the ping pong balls out, experiment with them. See what it takes to make them curve. Hit draws and fades. You can easily pick up little habits to take with you to the course.

-Rob Akins

3) Eleven Ball Drill

This drill was created by sports psychologist Dr. Rick Jensen. Chip eleven balls with the lie of the ball being wherever the ball drops. Chip to 2 or 3 different holes alternately until you have chipped all eleven balls. Take the five closest and the five farthest away which will leave you with the sixth ball, the median ball. Measure how far this ball is away from the hole and you now have your baseline. The Tour median is 1.5 feet. You work off of your personal best.

4) One Ball's Difference

Throw a sleeve of three balls onto the ground, and line them up facing the hole, one right next to the other. Line up as if the middle ball is normal ball position. Playing the ball that's farthest back will give you a lower shot with more run if you need it. Playing the forward ball will give you a slightly higher shot that will not run as much.

5) Take the Chipping Portion of the Red Zone Skills Test See page 14

Remember ...

1) When the ball is coming off the face too "hot," check your ball position. You are normally playing the ball too far back in your stance.

2) When the ball is coming off the face too "soft," you are normally playing the ball too far forward.

3) Think of this shot as a bump and run. Hitting it solidly is the bump. You control the bump and then feel how the ball runs. With practice this can be one of your best shots.

PICK THE CLUB YOU ARE COMFORTABLE WITH

When you are on the golf course, especially in a pressure situation, pick the club and shot type that you are most comfortable with. Many golf pundits would chastise Phil Mickelson for using his L-wedge to hit a flop shot when the simple shot seemed to be a low running shot. It was the right choice for Phil because that was his favorite shot, and the shot he was most comfortable with. He had a better chance of pulling this shot off than any other.

Until you have had a chance to practice some of our techniques to the point they are second nature, use the shot you are most comfortable with. Little by little, put the new shots into your repertoire.

USE YOUR HEAD

Chipping is a critical part of the game. And there's more to it than simply how close you get the ball to the hole.

If you don't chip the ball in, you want to chip it to the right spot. Way too many amateurs approach their chip shots with some vague idea of getting the ball somewhere in the vicinity of the hole, with no thought for putting the ball in the right position. Then they're left with tricky downhill four-footers, and they end up three-putting - all because they didn't think when they stood over their chip shot.

When chipping the ball, ask yourself this question: If this ball doesn't go in the hole, where do I want it to end up?

Pros understand this. It's rare that they leave themselves with a downhill putt after a chip shot. They know that a downhill left-to-right five footer is a lot tougher than a 12-foot uphill putt. You're much more likely to three-putt from above the hole; from below the hole, you have a legitimate chance to one-putt, and the worst you're going to do is two-putt.

Simply by thinking your way around the greens, you can save yourself four or five shots per round.

"How" to Practice Chipping

1. Use ping-pong balls or Almost Golf™ balls to practice indoors.

2. Pick your indoor drills and do them for short intervals for 6 days a week.

3. Do mirror work to make sure you have gotten rid of any "scooping" tendencies and have perfected an arc stroke.

4. Do your outdoor practice to targets and test yourself to monitor your progress. Use the chipping portion of the Red Zone test and the 11 Ball Test explained earlier.

Recommended Drills Prioritized for:

Silver Program

Solid Contact
1. Brush the Grass, Line
2. Look at Arms

Touch and Feel
1. Ping Pong Balls

Gold Program (Silver Program Drills Plus)

1. Punisher
2. 2X4 Drill

1. Take the Chip Test

Platinum Program (Previous Drills Plus)

1. Chip it in
2. Eleven Ball Drill

RED ZONE SUCCESS STORIES

Nancy Harvey

When Nancy entered t
Golf Academy her han
cap was around a 38
which tells you she
was at best right arour
the national averagє
for golfers.

NANCY HARVEY began her journey in golf playing recreationally with friends for a couple of years while she had a career in the business world. She didn't feel very fulfilled and decided in the fall of 1998 to enroll in the Golf Academy of the South (a two year occupational school for peo-ing a career in golf). When she entered the Golf Academy dicap was a around a 38, just above the national average for n this country. Her first tournament she shot a 128.

he Academy she met her first mentor and teacher Charlie s well as Brad Turner and staff. Her plan was to follow the ment side of the profession. She didn't feel like she could ever od enough player to pass the player ability test to become a rofessional. During her 16 months at the academy the stu-acher relationship developed and grew. They worked on ing every aspect of her game, from long game, course man-t, and especially short game.

cy says, "One of the most dramatic experiences I went was the short game skill testing. After the initial testing you iodically test yourself to monitor your progress. It is a sys-t has measurable progress and improvement, it is not sub-you either score better or you don't." She followed a program 1 100% improvement by the second testing.

This story almost didn't have a happy ending. In month she had a particularly bad tournament and was quit. She saw Charlie for a scheduled practice. "I'm just never going to be good enough," Nancy said as she held back the tears. "Nancy, you are going have to trust me and have faith. I have taken so many people through this process, I'll tell you the only thing I've seen keep a person from getting it." "What's that?" Nancy questioned. "Giving up," Charlie shot back. "Have faith and trust me, you are going to get this."

The next several months saw steady improvement until Nancy had her crowning achievement. As she was a month or two away from graduating, she shot a 78 in a tournament. Fifty shots better than her initial tournament score.

Nancy now has a career in golf. Her handicap has gone from 38 to 6 and she is a member of the LPGA Club Professional & Teaching Division. "Charlie helped to develop my passion for the game and teaching others. He has developed and is constantly try-ing to improve on measurable ways of improving your golf game. The testing and measuring that Charlie taught me at the academy is the same things that I use today still. The short game improve-ments allowed me to score better on the golf course and bring my handicap down. I understand that's part of what he and Rob are using for the Red Zone Challenge. It's very exciting that they are bring-ing this secret to everybody."

6

PITCHING

ONE OF THE PEOPLE

who had a strong influence on my teaching was a golf professional named Harry Obitz. Harry was an innovator in the golf business. He was one of the first people to start a golf school in the late '60s — he called it Swing's the Thing Golf School. He had a golf show that toured the world, and he once even appeared on the Ed Sullivan Show.

Harry would come to Orange Lake C.C. in Florida for the month of January each year during his retirement, and I took that opportunity to pick his brain. There were many things he told me, but the one that stands out to me as influencing my teaching philosophy the most was when he explained to me about swing methods. He said, "Charlie, I don't ever want to hear that you became a method teacher. All swing methods are glorified pitch shots."

This was 1989, and there were three methods that had a lot of popularity. Harry took each one and did a pitch shot version of the method. When he had finished, he made his point: Charlie, all a golf swing does is produce a ball flight. This is done because the skill and habits of the player, not because of a so-called scientifically better method. The problem with methods is that everyone regardless of their size has to fit into the same mold. But when you teach principles that build habits, a golfer's uniqueness can come out without sacrificing correct principles. So what I'm telling you is to teach principles, not meth-

> **" All swing methods are glorified pitch shots. "**

ods." I heeded Harry's advice and what he called principles I term Essentials.

The reason I feel this story is important to start this chapter is because if every method can be shown as a 'glorified pitch shot,' then learning to pitch the ball well not only helps your score but also gets you well on your way to a better full swing. It's our favorite two-for-one deal.
- Charlie King

Now let's map out the Pitching Essentials™ so you can improve on the golf course and lower your Red Zone handicap, while also improving your full swing in the process.

Grip

The grip has three purposes: 1) To hinge the club

The Pitching Essentials™

1. The Pre-Swing

The pre-swing is made up of three key elements: grip, aim, and set-up.

Grip

First, to correctly hinge the club, you should take the grip-end of the club and hold it only with the heel pad (which is placed on top of the grip) and the forefinger. You should then move the club up and down to check if the club is hinging properly. When you wrap your remaining three fingers around the club, you should see two or three knuckles on the left hand. If you see four knuckles, the grip is too strong; if you see no knuckles or just one knuckle, then the grip is too weak.

Next, you should place your right hand on the side of the club. The way you put your hands on the club allows you to achieve the second function of the grip, which is to square the clubface.

Now, take the club to the top of your backswing. Your left thumb and the pad of your right forefinger should support the club. If you are doing this with your grip, you now have a correct, functional grip.

There is a misunderstanding about light grip pressure. We like to see that the pressure in the arms and wrists is light and the fingers are snug on the club. This gives us the best of both worlds: speed from light arm and wrist pressure and support of the club through snug fingers on the club.

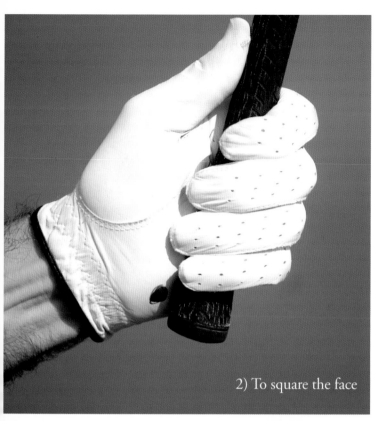

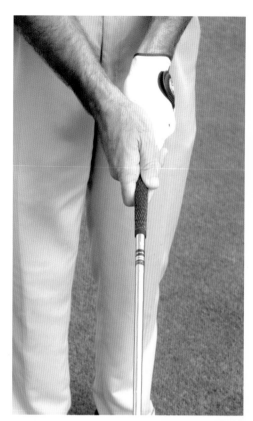

2) To square the face

3) To support the club at the top

Aim

Many players set up with their shoulders lined up to the target. This is another one of golf's misconceptions because, in reality, the player is now lined up to the right of the target. Because the clubface hits the ball, it only makes sense that you should line up your clubface with the target. A key principle to remember when going through your pre-shot routine is "clubface first, body second." Another key concept to remember is the shoulders are lined up parallel to and left of the target. The lower body should be lined up slightly left to create resistance for the backswing. This resistance creates a stopping point. Because players are standing sideways and dealing with visual distortion, it takes practice and feedback to become good at alignment.

Set-up

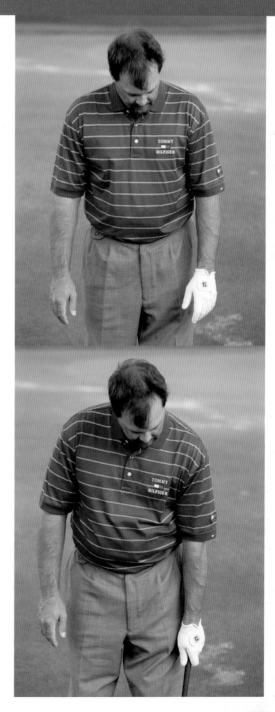

RED ZONE TIP

THE ANATOMIC DRILL

Stand tall and let your arms hang to your side. I like to call this the anatomic state. This is how God designed you. Make a fist with your left hand and look down. You should see two or three knuckles. If your hand is on the club in that position, you have a better chance of squaring up the clubface more often.

- Rob Akins

Posture

Why is good posture important? Because bad posture has three devastating effects: It restricts your arm movement; it restricts your body turn; and it leads to injuries.

When you stand straight, the back has a very small "s-shaped" curve. When you have good posture, the spine is healthy, and there should be a small gap between the vertebrae. Between vertebrae there is tissue called a disc, which acts as a cushion. When your posture gets slouched forward, the vertebrae touch, and the discs get squeezed and pinched. When this happens and you take your backswing, the vertebrae are grinding on each other and pinching the discs. This happens shot after shot, for years. The discs get inflamed and the back pain kicks in. Eventually you are unable to play because the pain is so severe.

So how do we avoid this? Well, one of the main principles in the set-up is to bend from the hips, not the waist. If you bend from the waist, your spine will be in the unhealthy position we just described. You must also have a slight knee flex to keep your weight balanced. This will get you in an athletic, balanced position to start your swing. We check this by giving you the "push" test. Once you take your posture, we give you a light push forward and backward to see that you are centered and cannot be pushed over easily. This allows you to learn to "feel" correct posture and weight distribution.

When you grip the club, your right hand is slightly lower than your left hand; corresponding to this, your right shoulder should be lower than your left. This slight tilt of the upper body we call "secondary angle." This secondary angle should be maintained throughout the golf swing.

Stance

Your feet should be shoulder width apart for most shots. The rule of thumb here is that a stance that is too narrow will cause you to lose balance easily, and a stance that is too wide will restrict your turn.

Ball Position

The best place to start in describing correct ball position is with the bottom of the arc. Every time we swing, the circle of our swing will have a point where the club shaft is vertical. This is the bottom of the arc. For iron shots the clubs needs to be descending to hit the ball in the sweet spot and have the loft get the ball up. Therefore, the ball needs to be behind the lowest point for this descent. A driver, on the other hand, needs to be struck with the club traveling level to slightly up. This ball needs to be placed opposite this lowest point. The low point of a correct swing will occur under the left arm (because if the left wrist is correctly flat approaching impact, the shaft is vertical under the left shoulder). Our guidelines for pitching ball position are as follows:

1. Good Lie Pitch Shot – under the sternum.
2. Mediocre or Bad Lie – just back of middle

USE BALL POSITION TO CONTROL THE ARC

In pitching, different distances call for different approaches. Depending on the amount of green you have to work with, your pitch shots may call for differing arc. Simply by using the ball position in your stance, you can control the arc and become a more accurate pitcher.

- When the ball is back in your stance, the arc is lower.
- When the ball is in the middle of your stance, the arc higher.
- When the ball is forward in your stance, the arc is h

Your position in relation to the ball also has an effect. The er you stand to the ball, the lower the arc (below, left).

A: Note the three ball positions. The arc of the ball depends on where you are in relation to the ball. B: The postition of the ball in your stance affects the arc as well.

2. Clubface Control

This is the often-overlooked essential that significantly controls the direction of the golf ball. We know that where a ball ends up is predominantly controlled by the clubface angle at impact. We know statistically that most golfers slice and are under the misconception that it is because they didn't take the club down the target line. Most golfers have no awareness of where the clubface is during their swing, which contributes largely to miss-hits. Following are a few key checkpoints to determine if you have your clubface in the correct position throughout your swing:

No: Toe Closed

No: Toe Open

1) From the address position, take your club back to parallel to the ground with the toe of the club up (but angled slightly to the right).

No: Shut Clubface

2) Continuing the back-swing will allow the club to begin to hinge, and the leading edge of the club should be in line with your left forearm.

3) Now, when the club starts down, the leading edge will be in a neutral position.

4) Finally, the handle will be leading to hit the ball solidly and the face will be pointed toward the target. The ball jumps off the loft of the face toward the target as you follow through to the "toe-up" position.

Too many times players will make an exaggerated attempt to take the club straight through, leaving the face pointing to the right of the path, creating side spin that hits the ball to the right. With correct instruction on clubface control, slicing could be eliminated altogether.

Imagine the face of a tennis racket and how you direct the ball with the face pointed right, left and straight.

3. Striking vs. Scooping

Ball-striking is a term used to describe the quality of contact between the golf ball and the clubface at impact. To describe the difference between a "strike" and a "scoop," I like to demonstrate by having a student slap my hand with their right hand. Invariably the contact is solid and flush with my right hand.

With a scooping motion (above), the weight stays back and the player tops the ball or hits too far behind it. The proper motion is a strike (top), not a scoop. Note the position of the striker's hands just after impact.

Striking is the hands and handle leaning slightly forward at contact with the weight on the left side. The bottom of the arc will be at or past the ball for solid shots. In my opinion, this is the number one fault in golf and very few know it. When a golfer is overheard saying, "I lifted my head on that one" or being told, "Keep your head down," you know they are operating under this widespread faulty concept. What we call the Strike is the movement and position that is the key to solid golf shots.

— Charlie King

The problem is that players do not know how to correctly use a lofted club. Because of the scooping motion in an attempt to "lift" the ball that many players make at impact, the player will either hit on top of the ball or well behind it. A correct strike of the ball will result in consistent ball flight and greater distance.

4. Pivot and Secondary Angle

This is the slight tilt in the spine caused by the right hand being lower than the left on the golf club at address. This angle should be monitored and maintained for a correct pivot. The most common fault in a golfer's body motion is the reverse pivot. This has been caused over the years by golfers being told to, "Keep your head still" but not being told what to do with their body. We have found that keeping this slight tilt consistent throughout the swing simplifies the pivot and makes it efficient.

The pivot is the way your body moves in the swing. It all starts in your posture. The secondary angle and forward bend from your hips are the angles around which your body rotates. The secondary angle becomes a great checkpoint. The shoulders should turn around the spine, avoiding any raising up or tilting down.

Weight shift is also an integral part of the pivot. There should be more weight on the right side in the backswing and more weight on the left in the forwardswing and finish. Because the body is turning and the arms are swinging on plane, weight shift is only one piece of the puzzle. When players incorrectly shift their weight, there are two common mistakes. First is a **"reverse pivot,"** (below) which we discussed earlier. Second, players may try to get their weight too much on the left side and will end up making excessive upper body movement to the right, resulting in their head being past their right foot. This movement is called a "sway."

In a reverse pivot, the weight shifts to the left side on the back-swing (above) and to the right side on the follow-through (below). This is a major swing flaw for many players.

5. Swinging the Club and Rhythm

We've talked about rhythm in putting, and it is just as critical pitching. Counting 'tick-tock' is a very effective drill to create go rhythm throughout your game. The reason we spend some time this subject is because it isn't as easy as it sounds. We mentioned go deadly instincts earlier, and they rear their ugly head to create qui tension-filled swings. Smooth, rhythmic swings are the go Another way to practice this is to count "one thousand one, one tho sand two" as you swing.

It is important to remember to let the laws of physics work your golf swing. Swinging more rhythmically and multiplying yo speed is only going to help you hit the ball more consistently.

6. Plane and Swing Arc

Swing plane has been misunderstood over the years, but one the key things to understand is the circle. When you take a club a swing as if the ball is teed up at your waist, you will see a horizon circle. We start to lower the spot where the imaginary ball is and t circle starts to tilt over until we get to ground level. We now have good feel and outline of a basic swing plane.

The golf club is built with an angle between the clubface and t shaft. It is not built like a croquet mallet or a pool cue, which wou go straight back and straight through. The angle that is creat means the club is most efficiently moved along a specific shape. T shape of the swing is what is known as swing plane. Swing plane i tremendous concept that, once pictured in your mind, shapes the w you swing and gives you an understanding of path.

"Straight back and straight through" is a misconception that lea to vertical backswings and out-to-in forwardswings. "Take the cl inside" has led to swings that are too flat on the backswing and o to-in on the forwardswing. An overall picture of the shape and sor key checkpoints are what will help you develop an on-plane swing

7. Width

Over the years, golfers have been told "Keep your left ar straight." This thought has been taken to mean stiffness in the arr The distance from the buttons on your shirt to the butt end of the cl should be maintained throughout the golf swing. This distance is t width in your swing and, just like the spokes on a wheel, it should st consistent throughout the swing.

Improvement begins with a golfer's concept of what he or s should do to have the best game. We have identified golf's major m conceptions and replaced them with the Seven Pitching Essenti that all golfers should know. Now we will show you some drills th will make these concepts second nature. In addition to developing yo ability to pitch the golf ball, you are also going to be making your fu swing better. The full-swing is simply a "glorified pitch." If you are ab to perfect the pitch, this will help your full swing tremendously.

Now that you are hitting the ball solidly, we need to examine wh determines how far the golf ball will go. The next chapter will he you with distance control.

In the pages that follow, we've referenced the applicab pitching essential with each drill.

Pitching Drills

1) Line Drill

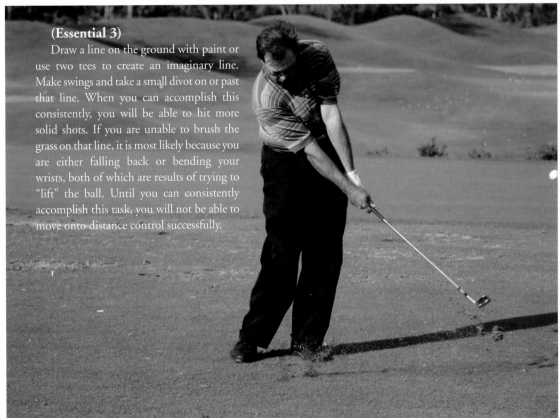

(Essential 3)

Draw a line on the ground with paint or use two tees to create an imaginary line. Make swings and take a small divot on or past that line. When you can accomplish this consistently, you will be able to hit more solid shots. If you are unable to brush the grass on that line, it is most likely because you are either falling back or bending your wrists, both of which are results of trying to "lift" the ball. Until you can consistently accomplish this task, you will not be able to move onto distance control successfully.

2)
Impact
Bag

(Essentials 2, 3)

Golf's best all around training aid. Pop the impact bag and you will see the hands lead and face square. Get the feeling that the bag "jumps" away from the clubface. Give the bag a healthy "pop".

3) Pivot Drill

(Essential 4)

Look in a mirror and check your set-up (keys for set-up are earlier in the chapter).

a. While looking face-on into the mirror, maintain the slight spine tilt as you turn.

b. While looking at the side view, make your turn with your shoulders maintaining a 90-degree angle relative to your spine bent forward.

4) Circle Tilted Over

(Essential 6) Take your Sand Wedge and start out swinging as if the ball is teed up at your waist. This will result in a circular swing that is horizontal like a merry-go-round. Next, lower the circle as if the ball is teed up at your knees. This will result in your circle tilting over on more of a diagonal plane. Now go to ground level and make your circular swing. This creates an attitude of a whole motion instead of so many parts and a great swing plane.

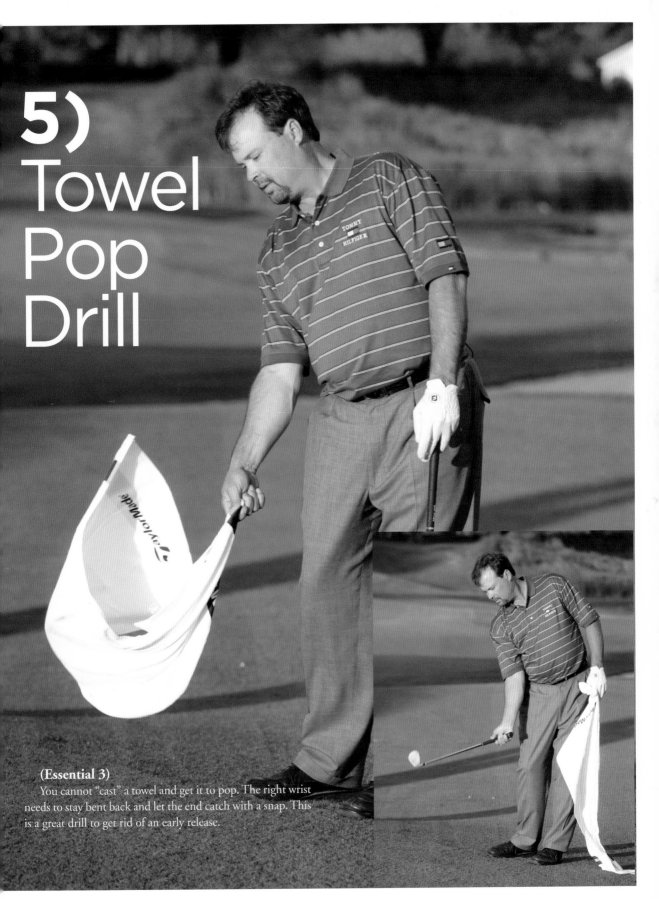

5) Towel Pop Drill

(Essential 3)

You cannot "cast" a towel and get it to pop. The right wrist needs to stay bent back and let the end catch with a snap. This is a great drill to get rid of an early release.

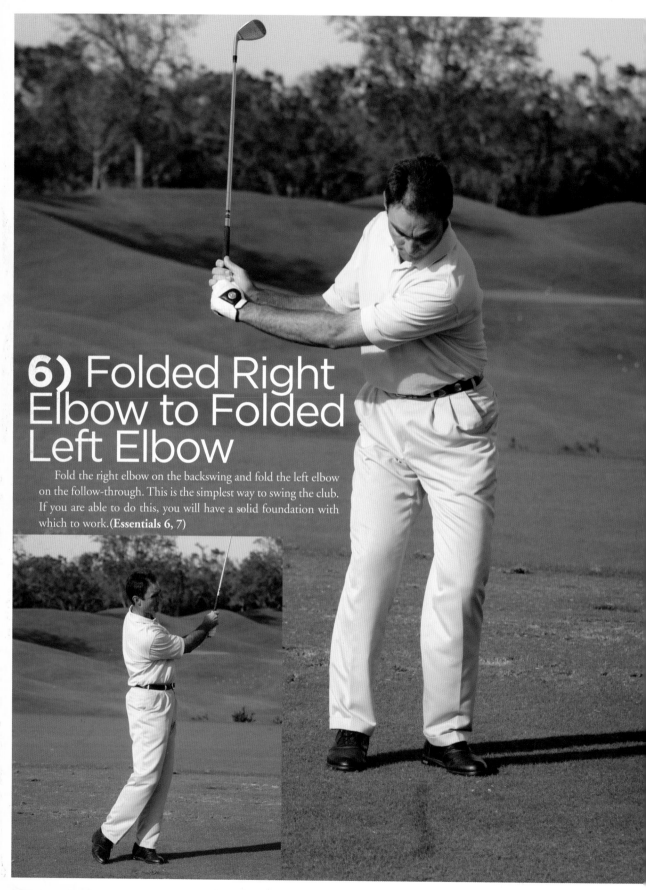

6) Folded Right Elbow to Folded Left Elbow

Fold the right elbow on the backswing and fold the left elbow on the follow-through. This is the simplest way to swing the club. If you are able to do this, you will have a solid foundation with which to work. (**Essentials 6, 7**)

7a) Lag Drill

7b) Hinge and Lag Drill

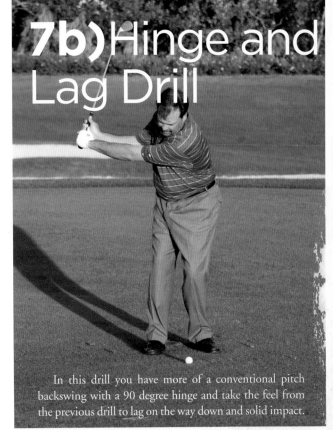

On this drill you will have a late hinge going back to give you the feel of lagging the wrist coming down. Another drill to get rid of an early release.

In this drill you have more of a conventional pitch backswing with a 90 degree hinge and take the feel from the previous drill to lag on the way down and solid impact.

7c) Hinge to Rehinge

Make a half-swing, focusing on the hinging and rehinging of the wrists. This will allow you to create maximum clubhead speed with minimal effort.

8) Three Finger Curl Down

The three-finger curl down is a great drill if you are scooping or slicing — or both. This drill counteracts the upward tendency of a Scooper and creates the downward hit of a Striker. Take a club halfway back and then start the club down while feeling the last three fingers of the left hand "curl down." As you curl the last three fingers down, the left wrist also arches out. This is what the late Claude Harmon used to refer to as "Bethlehem Steel" at impact. "You want to have Bethlehem steel at impact son, no linguine," Mr. Harmon would exhort. Do this drill as part of your 5 minutes to Better Golf™ and you will be on the road to solid, straight shots.

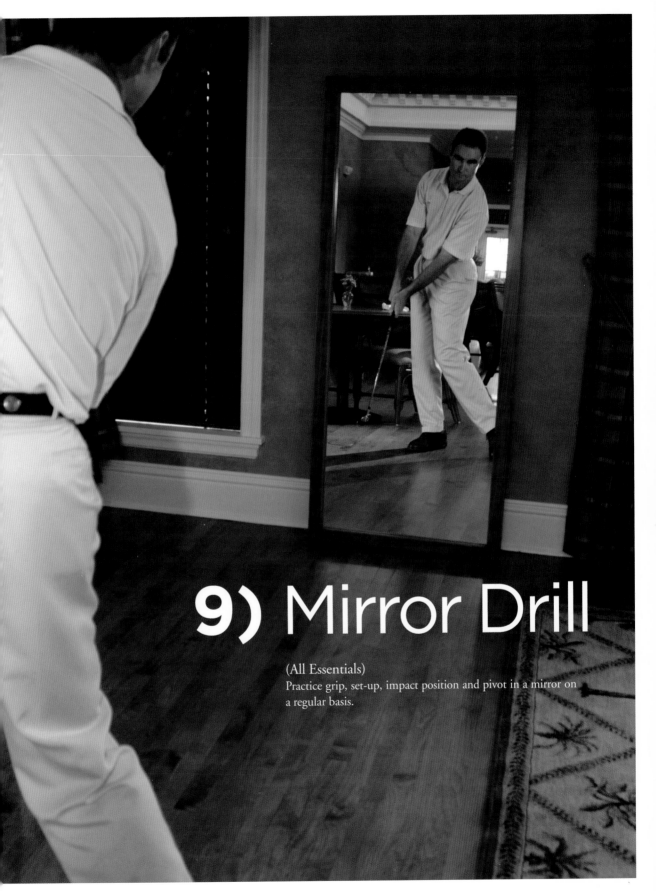

9) Mirror Drill

(All Essentials)
Practice grip, set-up, impact position and pivot in a mirror on
a regular basis.

"How" to Practice Pitching

1. 5 Minutes to Better Golf™ exercises to do at home:
   a. Mirror Drill practicing grip, posture and pivot in the mirror.
   b. Practice the three-finger curl down drill described earlier.
   c. Circle tilted over and swing plane work in a mirror to perfect your arc for pitching.
   d. Make small "swings" and count tick-tock to yourself to establish great rhythm.
2. Outdoor should be plenty of Line Drill work. Also, pick your favorites from our list.
3. Test yourself in this category every 4 weeks

Recommended Drills
Prioritized for:

Silver Program

1. Line Drill
2. Impact Bag
3. Pivot Drill
4. Mirror Drill

Gold Program (Silver Program Drills Plus)

1. Circle Tilted Over
2. Towel Pop Drill
3. Folded Right Elbow to Folded Left Elbow
4. Lag Drill

Platinum Program (Previous Drills Plus)

1. Hinge to Rehinge Drill
2. Hinge and Lag Drill

Putting It All Together

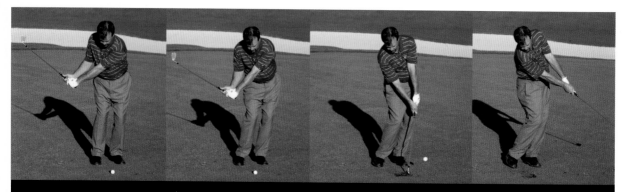

The full swing is simply a "glorified pitch." If you perfect the pitch, you're on your way to perfecting the full swing.

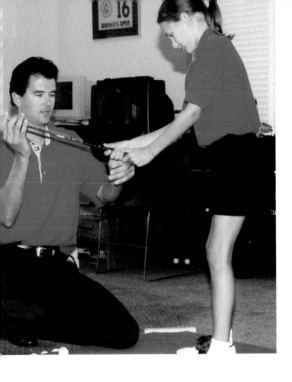

RED ZONE SUCCESS STORIES

Carroll Clark

Although I never played on the PGA Tour as I thought I would after my first par, **golf** has become a big part of my daily life."

ARROLL PLAYED GOLF FOR the first time in the fall of 1991 after returning from a Marine unit in Operation Desert Storm. He was 24 years old and not sure what his next step in life was. Over the next couple of years, he got a bug for golf in a big way and decided to make it a career.

first met Charlie King in August of 1993 at the Golf ly of the South in Casselberry, Florida. He entered the acad- the fall semester with a 17 handicap. And with the help of and the staff, he graduated in December of 1994 with a 5 p. He and Charlie set quantifiable goals that were monitored "Charlie was different from other teachers I had taken les- om in the past. We set goals and developed a plan. Charlie ed if I followed the plan my short game handicap would go nd their for my scores would go down. He was right in both stances."

12 weeks during his first semester he followed this routine. day and Wednesday – Chipping and Putting utted 100 putts on Mondays and Wednesdays from three ween two 2x4, he also putted 10 balls from 10, 20, 30, 40 feet to develop feel for distance. "I remember Charlie stat- most three putts are caused by a poor first putt, not a poor

second putt." He chipped 25 balls to a short flag, 25 balls to a medium flag, 25 balls to a long flag and 25 balls to alternating flags for feel.

Tuesday and Thursday – Pitching and Bunker Play

He pitched 10 balls from 20, 40, 60, 80, and 100 yards to towels he laid out on the range. Carroll also used this time to worked on his alignment with two clubs laid down and used his pre-shot routine for each shot. He also went into the bunker and hit fifty balls from different lies.

His short game handicap went from 21 down to 4 in 12 weeks. Through Charlie and the staff's teaching techniques and Carroll's hard work, he had totally changed his short game and his self-confidence in his game from 100 yards and in.

"Now 11 years later I teach these short game skills to my students and I see the difference every day. One of my junior students Tyler Smith just won the National Drive, Chip and Putt in his age division. Although I never played on the PGA Tour as I thought I would after my first par, golf has become a big part of my daily life. I am now a PGA Member, Division I College Golf Coach and Director of the Tennessee PGA Junior Golf Academy. I run an Elite Junior Camp with Rob Akins each summer and introduced Rob and Charlie. These two together spend every working moment figuring out ways to simplify golf and motivate golfers. Take the Red Zone Challenge. You'll be glad you did."

7

WEDGES

DISTANCE CONTROL
FROM 30 – 100 YARDS

I HAD A LESSON

with top teacher Craig Shankland in 1991. "Golfers in the '50s and '60s were more accurate than golfers today," he told me. I said, "Come on, Craig, you're just partial to the era you came up in." Craig shot back (in his distinctive English accent): "No, Charlie. I'll tell you why golfers were more accurate then. We hit to living, breathing targets called caddies. At each Tour event there was a field designated for practice and the player's caddy shagged balls for his player."

I said, "Craig, I know that. But how do you think that led to more accuracy?"

Craig replied, "There were no sloppy shots. It was a source of pride that your caddy moved very little. Hogan's caddy would catch one-hoppers all day. Palmer's caddy might take a step. When I first got on Tour, my caddy was sprinting to catch up with the balls I was hitting." Craig then mimicked his unfortunate caddy running from side to side while watching for the ball like a baseball outfielder.

"Because of the embarrassment and because we all wanted to be like Hogan, Nicklaus and Palmer, we focused in on the badge of honor of one-hopping all of our golf balls to our caddies. This natural laser beam focus made us better."

Later in the chapter we outline a drill that came from this story, the "Happy Caddy" game. The laser beam focus of hitting to definite targets is a big factor in becoming good in this part of your game.

- Charlie King

The ball-striking principles we touched on in the last chapter are especially useful with a wedge in your hand. And when we talk wedges, we're talking distance control above all else.

> " The laser beam focus of hitting to definite targets is a big factor in becoming good in this part of your game. "

Studies have shown that getting up and down in the 30- to 100-yard range has the biggest correlation to your score and overall success. There are several reasons this is true. To hit it close enough to get up and down, you have be a good ball-striker, and to make the putts you need to make, you obviously have to be a good putter.

There are a couple of ways to approach wedges, and both can be successful. We recognize that each golfer is unique, and not everyone will do things the same way. Some players perform better with a more structured approach, and for you we are going to give you a definitive system. For the more feel-oriented players, we are going to talk about how to practice and think to become more consistent in your distance control.

The Structured Approach

You are a structured golfer if you tend to analyze things a little bit more deeply, and if having a system sounds like a good idea. (If you don't know whether or not you're a structured player, give this approach a try first, and you'll find out.) For you we are going to recommend controlling the length and speed of your swing to control your distance.

Here's something that's perfect for the structured golfer: the Clock Image System. Picture your swing from face on as a clock, with six o'clock at your feet and 12 o'clock at your head, with your left arm as the hands of the clock. When we talk about a 9 o'clock position, for example, we are talking about the left arm position, not the club position.

Another way to think of this: In the body parts system, you use the knees, hips and shoulders as your reference point. An example would be a hip high backswing to a shoulder high follow through to hit a 60-yard shot.

Drill — Take a sand wedge and set up a couple of targets where you know the distance (i.e. 25 and 50 yards). Hit ten shots with a 9 o'clock backswing and a follow-through to 2 or 3 o'clock. Notice where the ball lands when hit solidly. This becomes your baseline distance.

Most golfers go out onto the course totally guessing, but you can go out there with confidence in certain distances. For example, standing over a 50-yard shot and knowing it is your 9 o'clock swing will make a huge difference in your results.

As you start to master the 9 o'clock swing, do a 10 o'clock swing for a longer distance and an 8 o'clock swing for a shorter distance.

The next part of the equation is the speed you use within the length of swing. A long swing with slow speed can produce a high, soft shot. The 9 o'clock swing can hit it various distances with slow, medium or maximum speed. Generally we want you to use the medium speed as your normal speed.

What the pros do, and what you should do, is to change the rhythm of the swing to match the shortened backswing on a partial wedge shot. For a pro, each backswing takes the same amount of time, whether it's a 30-yard pitch with a short backswing, or a 60-yard pitch with a longer backswing. In other words, a pro takes the club back more slowly on a shorter swing. It takes the same amount of time to execute a half-backswing as it does a three-quarter backswing.

Several studies have shown that with most professional players, the backswing takes three times longer than from the top of the swing to impact, no matter the length of the shot. It's the same thing on a pitch shot. If you want to accelerate properly through the shot, take the club back slowly, and then it's easier to accelerate. Good rhythm is the key.

(RED ZONE TIP)
THE INNER METRONOME
As we mentioned for pitching in the last chapter, we want you to continue to count to yourself as you swing. Saying "tick, tock" evenly or "thousand-one, thousand-two" promotes a rhythmic swing that stands up under pressure and gives you consistent results.

With a lot of practice, this will become natural for you, and you'll see a huge improvement in your partial wedges. And that masterful touch you see from the Tour players, that touch that seems so natural, will be yours.

9 o'clock backswing

8 o'clock backswing

3 o'clock follow-through

Real World Example

Jim figures out his 9 o'clock swing with a sand wedge is 55 yards. The same swing with his pitching wedge goes 70 yards. With his 60-degree wedge the ball goes 40 yards. One swing, three different clubs and some of the most common distances covered. He does the some thing with a 10 o'clock swing and an 8 o'clock swing. He's got all his key distances covered.

What he finds over time is that he has so much confidence in his sand wedge, he uses it by modifying the speed of his swing off of his baseline distance. For a 40-yard shot he does his 9 o'clock swing with a slower speed. Jim has created his own system, but it all started by knowing his 9 o'clock swing distance with a sand wedge.

The Feel Approach

We hear a lot of golfers say they can do it well by feel. They just look at it and somehow they know how far to hit it. The only problem is that many times, their test scores don't bear it out. We will not allow someone to say they are a feel player. They have to prove it to us during a Red Zone test. Once we feel certain that we have a golfer who can just see it, feel it, and do it, we practice hitting to targets to sharpen their sense of feel.

It makes sense that you could be successful this way because we can toss a ball to a target 20 feet away or 40 feet away without knowing exactly how far to swing club back and through. You simply react to your target based on practice.

How to Practice for the Feel Player

We challenge this golfer and get them to challenge themselves. Not only do we pick targets, but we also create situations (imaginary bunkers, water hazards and the like on the range). We want to see if there is a situation that the golfer can conquer in a different way if necessary. The feel golfer needs to pick very specific targets and see how close they can get it to these targets.

DISTANCE WEDGES: FILL IN THE GAPS

I'm going to say something radical. If you're playing a ball that is marketed as being for distance, then you're giving up four to six shots per round. The reason? The equipment you're using is more than likely a poor match for the ball you're striking.

If you're not paying attention to the lofts of your clubs, you're asking for trouble. Many of today's pitching wedges are lofted at 45 degrees — that's yesteryear's 8-iron. Today's gap wedge is yesterday's pitching wedge.

Let me put it this way. As an amateur player you rely heavily on your shorter clubs to save strokes. Say you hit a poor drive on a par 4 and have to punch it into the fairway. You're left with a 115-yard third shot into the green, and you need to get it within six feet to have a good shot at saving par.

Well, you're hitting a distance ball that's tough to control with a club that is lofted differently from what the shot calls for. It's a recipe for failure.

In other words, there's a gap in your equipment where you can least afford it. Tour players know this; that's why they carry a bunch of wedges that cover them in these situations. They understand the delicate balance between distance and control. If that's true for the pros, then it's doubly true for you amateur players. If you're like many amateurs and only hit five or six greens in regulation per round, then it's critical to carry the right wedges with the right lofts, and to play a ball that responds on the greens.

- Rob Akins

"How" to Practice Distance Wedges

1. When you feel like you have made a habit of hitting the ball solidly, you want to start to focus on your system of touch or do it by feel.

2. Set up a target at a known distance. Hit 10 shots at a time to that target to see if there is a pattern.

3. Monitor your rhythm constantly — it is critical to Red Zone success.

Putting It All Together

The Happy Caddy Game

For this one you need a partner. This game came from the story at the beginning of the chapter from top teacher Craig Shankland.

It dawned on me that this could be used as a practice principle, and you can use it, too. Find a partner and play the 'Happy Caddy' Game. You get to use one ball. One player stays in place while the other moves to different distances as you hit the ball back and forth to each other. When the ball is one-hopped to your partner, he is the 'Happy Caddy.' When you chunk it short or skull it long and your caddy has to run to get it, he is unhappy. This way of practicing creates focus like no other.

8

BUNKERS

THE "THUMP" VS. THE "THUD"
THE SECRETS TO GREAT BUNKER PLAY

ULIUS BOROS WAS A GREAT

champion, but he had to overcome his fear to earn his greatest victory. Specifically, it was his fear of bunkers that held him back at the 1962 U.S. Open. That fear kept him from aiming at flags and hitting it close.

Boros proceeded to spend a year on the beach, as it were. For the next year, he spent part of every day working on his sand play. Gradually, he became comfortable with his bunker shots and got the point where he truly excelled in the sand.

By the time the 1963 U.S. Open rolled around, Boros' bunker-phobia had evaporated. He was able to go after flags fearlessly. He went on to win the 1963 Open in a playoff with Arnold Palmer and Jacky Cupit, and he credited his fear of bunker practice with giving him the necessary confidence.

Want to know the ironic thing? That weekend, he didn't hit his ball into a single bunker. It's not so surprising, really. Once he conquered his fear of bunkers, his swing was more aggressive and confident and he hit every green.

- Rob Akins

> " To hit consistent bunker shots, you need to take long, shallow divots and hit the sand in the same spot each time. "

Today's the day you conquer your fear of bunkers.

Many PGA Tour pros will tell you in their magazine and TV tips that the bunker shot is the easiest in golf. This is pretty demoralizing when you are having difficulty even getting the ball out of the bunker, much less near the hole.

Well, guess what? Those pros are wrong. Our short game skill testing data has shown us that the bunker shot is the hardest shot in golf for most amateurs.

Rather than let that fact defeat you, we challenge you to make it a positive. Because of the initial high scores that you're likely to post in your Red Zone skills test, bunker play has the potential for the most noticeable improvement of any shot in your Red Zone arsenal.

So, what do these touring professionals know that makes the bunker shot so easy for them? You're about to find out.

The sand wedge is designed differently than any other club in your bag, thanks to Gene Sarazen, who got an inspiration while watching millionaire Howard Hughes work the controls of his airplane. "I was trying to make myself a club that would drive the ball up as I drove the club down," Sarazen said. "When a pilot wants to take off, he doesn't raise the tail of his plane, he lowers it. Accordingly, I was lowering the tail of my niblick to produce a club whose face would come up from the sand as the sole made contact with the sand." This idea led him to put solder on the back of a niblick (which was like our 9-iron) so it would skid through the sand instead of dig. He tried many different combinations until he found one he liked. He is given credit with inventing the first true sand wedge in 1931.

The 'bounce' of a sand wedge is what allowed us to start playing the shot differently. Before the sand wedge came along, the player could try to chip it out or hit it fat with a big swing. Hitting under it on purpose is what we do today, but it was not reliable because the club would dig in the sand instead of skid.

That's the genius of the sand wedge. The bottom of the club, known as bounce, is lower than the leading edge. This allows the club to skid through the sand and not dig too deep.

I know that sounds simple, but it can make a profound difference in your bunker play.

The Bunker Essentials™

In the bunker, it's easy to get sidetracked by things that are not essential. You've heard it before: Line up left, swing left, open the face and hit two inches behind the ball. Though there is truth in each of these statements, they take you away from the essential task in the bunker: Take a long, shallow divot in the bunker with the ball in the middle of that divot.

You should open the face slightly to create more 'skid' or 'bounce.' But we want you to line up parallel for the time being until the ball goes right of the target consistently. Then, and only then, should you line up to the left of the target. By focusing your attention on the most critical thing — the long, shallow divot — you will be able to master and understand bunker play thoroughly.

The reason we don't like the thought "Hit two inches behind it" is because you can accomplish that task and still go too deep and not get the ball out of the bunker. When you take that eight or nine inch shallow divot with ball in the middle of that divot, the ball flight is high and soft every time.

When practicing, all the divots you take in the sand should begin at the same place. You will need to become consistent in doing this just as you have become consistent in taking a divot at the same spot when hitting out of the fairway.

Find a practice bunker and take a few swings, knocking some sand out of the bunker. Notice how far the sand flies, where the divot starts and the sound of the club hitting the sand. Was the divot long and shallow? Are your divots starting behind the center of your stance? Does the contact with the sand sound like a pleasing "thump" or a jarring "thud"? (A "thump" would be the good one).

Once you are controlling your divots of sand, place a ball slightly ahead of the middle of your stance. Stay focused on the divot of sand as if the ball is a large speck of sand. Make the same swing, taking the long, shallow divot of sand, which will explode the ball onto the green. **Your success will be contingent on your ability to take the same long, shallow divot and start the divot in the same place.**

Thinking of it this way, distance control is relatively easy. Make the sand fly short, medium and long distances to hit short, medium and long bunker shots. You can control the distance with the length and speed of your swing.

Putting these ideas into practice will change your success in the bunker. Maybe you will be able to say it's the easiest shot in golf.

Keys and Drills

There are several keys and drills that we follow in order to help you become a more consistent player. Keep reading.

1) Set up

a) Set up a little lower. Dig your feet in to get a solid base. Your swing will now end up going down into the sand.
b) Ball positioned just in front of middle
c) Weight center to slightly left

2) Bunker boards

Use "bunker boards" to get a sense of the club skidding through the sand. Early success with this will eliminate the fear of the bunker shot. Place a 1"x6" board in the sand. Put a scoop of sand on top of the board with a ball on top of the sand. Knock sand off the board, and watch the ball "explode" out.

3) Line Drill

This line drill is a little different than the one we used for pitching. Draw a line in the sand. If the long, shallow divot is roughly eight inches long, half of if should be before the line and half of it after the line. Practice hitting bunker shots without the ball to consistently hit the same spot and to develop a feel for the explosion effect of the sand.

To help you practice taking a consistent divot of sand, draw lines around your divot for guidance. You should develop the same long, shallow divot that starts and ends in the same place each time.

Use the length and speed of your swing to control the length of your bunker shot.

4) Take a Divot and Watch the Sand Fly

Taking a long, shallow divot and watching the sand fly onto the lip of the bunker gives you a sense of how the club propels sand and, therefore, the ball. Remember: Make sure the divot is long and shallow and is right between your feet.

WILLISTON PARK PUBLIC LIBRARY

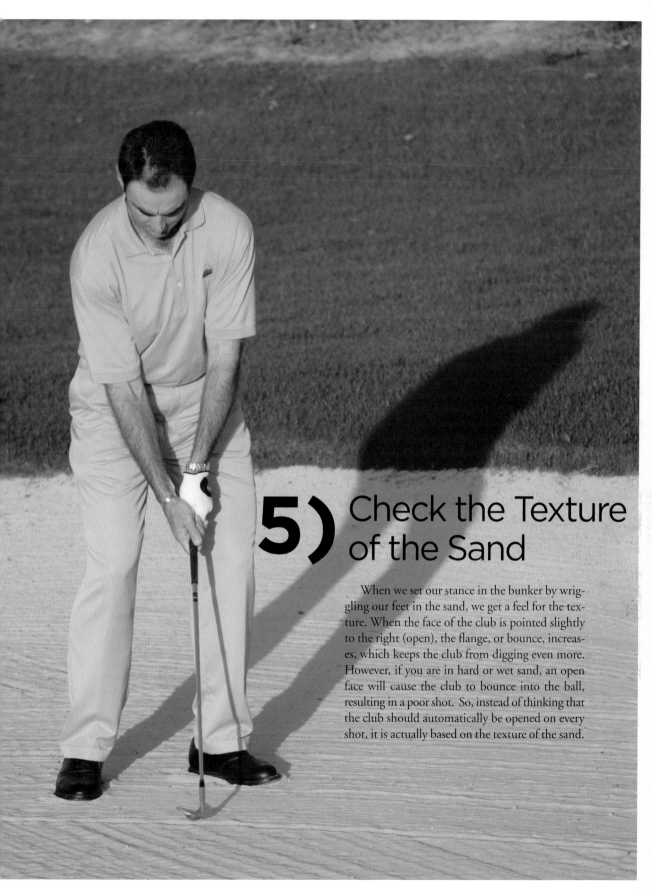

5) Check the Texture of the Sand

When we set our stance in the bunker by wriggling our feet in the sand, we get a feel for the texture. When the face of the club is pointed slightly to the right (open), the flange, or bounce, increases, which keeps the club from digging even more. However, if you are in hard or wet sand, an open face will cause the club to bounce into the ball, resulting in a poor shot. So, instead of thinking that the club should automatically be opened on every shot, it is actually based on the texture of the sand.

Trouble Bunker Shots
Buried Lies, Footprints, Fried Eggs, etc.

There are several keys that need to be considered when playing a bunker shot with a buried lie. First, the club needs to dig instead of skid when hitting the ball. You need to close the clubface slightly and make a more up and down swing. In addition to this, you should not have a very big follow-through. Finally, the ball will come out because of the explosion of sand with very little spin — therefore, the ball will roll much further than a good lie bunker shot. Check the photo sequence below to see how this is done.

(RED ZONE TIP)

DISTANCE CONTROL
The Longer the Shot, the Longer the Follow-Through

After 20 years of study, I've decided that the best way to control distance is to control your follow-through. The longer the shot, the longer the follow-through. All the other elements of the stroke remain the same. And don't be afraid on longer bunker shots to try a different club. If you open a 9-iron, it has bounce like a sand wedge, but it will carry, release and run farther. It's a great help on the long explosion shot, which is the riskiest shot in golf.

- Rob Akins

It's simple. The longer the shot, the longer the follow-through. Continued on next page

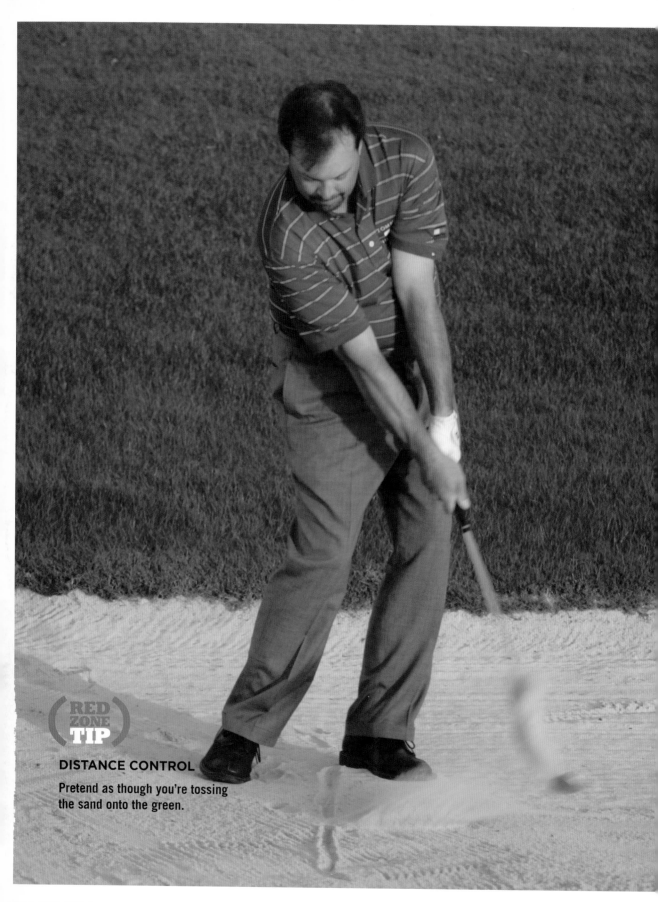

DISTANCE CONTROL

Pretend as though you're tossing
the sand onto the green.

RED ZONE TIP

DISTANCE CONTROL
For a longer toss, you'd use a longer follow-through, right?

"How" to Practice Bunker Play

1. The key here is to establish a long, shallow divot in the right place before introducing the ball.

2. When the divot is established, start to hit balls out on that same established divot. Notice if the sound stays the same. If you are doing it correctly, the ball will come out high and soft with little run. If you are hitting too far behind it, the ball will come out low and run.

3. Build confidence through success and test yourself to see how you are doing.

PRACTICE MAKES PERMANENT

PUT IN A PHONE CALL

o Dr. Rick Jensen, a sports psychologist whom I had met sev-
ral years before. "Rick, I'm putting together a program for the
Golf Academy of the South and I want your input," I told him.
Fire away," he answered.

"I'm not happy with the typical paradigm of teaching where a
rson signs for a single lesson and hopes for a miracle. It's not like
at in any other sport."

"You're right, Charlie. Golf is operating on an old way of think-
g that needs to be changed," Rick said. I could hear the passion in
s voice, so I knew I was onto something.

"I want to create a program that becomes the model for learning
is game and creating a higher success rate," I said. "From your per-
ective as a motor learning guy, what are the steps to create this pro-
am?"

"The first step is to create the hierarchy
skills," Rick replied.

"That's a nice, big ten-dollar word.
hat's that?"

"It's you thinking about golf and
ciding what's the most important
ill, and then the next and the next.
nce you have your hierarchy, then
u start to create the program."

That conversation started a
ought process that led to the pro-
am you are getting in this book today.
correct approach to setting out "how"
is game is learned most effectively and
ficiently. The Hierarchy of Skills that I used
create this program is in the Appendix for
ose who are curious to see the order I came up with.

- Charlie King

You need a plan. We all need a plan, whether it's golf, person-
finances or our health. We can have it explained one hundred
fferent ways, but if we aren't given the steps, most of us won't do
. If you follow the plan mapped out in this book on a daily basis,
u will have a great chance of playing the kind of golf you are capa-
e of.

In the past, you would get a "How-to" book or video or maybe

> You have the opportunity to become somewhere between good and great at a game you can enjoy for a lifetime.

a lesson and you would only get the "what" of learning golf. That
approach teaches "fundamentals" — the grip, aim, set-up, swing
plane, impact, short game, etc. This has been confusing because the
premise in marketing is to be different. To differentiate ourselves as
teachers, we have had decades of competition to come up with the
latest fad teaching method. It is no different than the fad diets that
come and go. In order to differentiate, these methods have confused
the golfer. We didn't want to fall into that trap in this book. The way
we broke down the "What" in this book is by skill, in order of
importance.

But what about the "How", the "How
much", the "When", with "Who" or
even the "Where"? These details being
left out have made golf even more
complicated. How could you possibly
know "How," "What," "When" and
"Where" to practice? What order
should I learn golf? How much time
should I spend per day? What type of
teacher should I have help me?
Doing what? Great questions and
finally answered for you in the previous
chapters in this book.

"This has happened in other sports
and activities. Learning the piano is not a
mystery. There are certain skills that are taught
as you progress through your books and lessons. Learning to swim
is one of my favorite analogies. If I was going to teach you to swim,
I would not throw you into the deep end and say "Sink or swim."
If that's how you learned to swim, though, it's doubtful that you would
be effective and efficient. You would learn to dog paddle to keep your
head above water and propel yourself to the side. Instead I would
take you to the shallow end of the pool, get you accustomed to the
water and teach you to float. You would then be shown how to kick
your legs properly for efficiency and then arm motion and breathing. We would put it all together in the shallow end with your

instructor nearby. When I feel like you have gained the confidence you need to swim without assistance, we would go to the deep end to show that you can swim in any depth of water."

- Charlie King

This analogy has many of the elements we are looking for in golf instruction. The main one we want to point out is the iden- ification of skills and building the learning process around those skills. Golf can be broken down in the same way by its main skills. By definition if you are becoming more skillful, you are a better golfer. Golf's version of floating is Pre-swing; grip, aim and setup. This has been modeled for you in the pictures in the Skills pters and you will be putting in only a few 5 Minutes to Better M exercises a day to make it into a habit. The leg kick in swim- synonymous with Face Control and Striking the ball in ipping and putting. Controlling the face is the domi- the direction of the ball and learning to Strike the key to satisfying contact. Our version of the arm ing for pitching, chipping, and bunker play is hm, and Efficient Body Movement. Once these Skills ed, you will do the "reps" to turn them into habits. W u e reps because we all know that to build a muscle you must put your reps in. And it is an absolute certainty that your scles will grow and get stronger if you do your repetitions cor- ly and with progressively more weight. It is just as certain in that when you do your reps for the particular Skill that you in your game the skill becomes second nature.

You have an opportunity to become somewhere between good reat at a game that you can enjoy for a lifetime. Be willing to the relatively short period of time to build the habits that you make your golf experience second to none. Our 12 week pro- um is designed to give simple, profound distinctions that make all difference in the world between success and failure. You get to oose your time commitment level. We know how busy you all are. ut for some of you, this is your profession, and we've set out to cre- ate a book and program whose principles are sound for all levels of golfers and can be used by all skill levels.

The Commitment Process

Follow the directions below to create a strong enough "why," a strong enough purpose. Improving in the short game is no different than losing weight or saving for retirement. These are all things we intend to do but somehow don't get around to it. The reason we maybe have not gotten around to it is we didn't go through a process to know our purpose or "why."

Many times pain leads to a strong "why". A person who has a heart attack goes on a strict diet and exercises religiously. This per- son has a life or death "why." Diet and exercise or else. Two things motivate us: pleasure and pain. We can get our purpose for the Challenge from the positive aspect of improving, or we can pic- ture some of our short game failures in crucial situations to get the pain to motivate us.

Commitment Steps

1. Decide "why" you want to complete the Challenge. The m vivid the reason the better. Create a positive "why" and a negat "why." This will give you twice as much of a chance to complete program. Example: The positive "why" could be picturing the lov scores and the ability to make pars when it matters. The negat "why" could be remembering your past failures every time y think about skipping a practice during your Challenge.

2. Write it down. Things that are written down elicit a dee commitment and a better chance of following through.

3. Refer back to it on a regular basis, especially when you feel yo commitment slipping.

Red Zone Practice Keys

1. Consistent practice is better than a long practice session ev once in a while.

2. Follow the program and have trust that the improvement w take place. Be patient, especially in the early stages.

3. There are two types of practice: **technique** and **compet tion**. When you are improving your skills and building habits, y are working on your technique. This type of practice requires a l of repetitions. Competitive practice is putting the ball in the hole as few strokes as possible or beating a personal best in a category. Th can be games where you compete against your personal best where you compete against your friends. Many golfers wonder wl their practice doesn't seem to translate to better scores, and a lack competitive practice is usually why.

More Competitive Games

1) Ben Hogan Game — This is a putting game so name because of Hogan's reputation as a great ball-striker. If you hit all greens in regulation, what would you shoot? Do this on a practi green. You have a birdie putt on every hole and you putt six sho putts (four to six feet), six medium putts (ten to twenty feet) and s long putts (25 to 35 feet). Keep track of your personal best ar compete against a friend. You can also play nine-hole games to tal less time.

2) Seve Game — Seve Ballesteros was known for his imagin tive short game and especially later in his career, his erratic fu swing. If you missed all nine greens in regulation on your front nin what would you shoot? At a short game area, assume you are ne the green in regulation and you will get par with an up-and-dow Mix it up between chips, short pitches and bunker shots and ha three easy shots, three medium shots and three hard shots. After yo have hit your shot toward the hole, you can mark your putt just you would on the course. Use your imagination to make these sit ations just as real as they would be on the course.

10

CHOOSING A TEACHER

What To Look for in an Instructor or Golf School

WHEN I WAS FIVE

years old, my daddy bought me a putter and a 4-wood. My backyard was the 16th hole of a municipal course in Shreveport, Louisiana. The course was at times my babysitter with afternoons spent hitting that 4-wood and putting on the green. I had pretty good hand-eye coordination and learned to hit that 4-wood without any instruction. From ages six to 11, I raced and took care of quarter horses. This takes a lot of time, so I was just dabbling at golf.

When I was 11, I got serious about golf. I practiced all the time. I took a lesson from the pro where I played. He was a respected player and he gave me great advice, "Take the Driver, 3-wood and 3-iron out of your bag. Tee off with your 5-wood or 5-iron and become the best chipper and putter in the city." I chipped and putted for hours and won the city championship in my age division for three straight years.

At 13 I decided to change my swing. After my lessons, I couldn't even hit the ball. My teacher got frustrated with me and quit teaching me. I decided to go on a quest to learn the best swing and could not find the answers in Shreveport.

By 15 I had figured a lot out by trial and error and knew I was going to be a player. The bad thing was I kept experimenting and that hurt my game. I was a good player — just not the great player I set out to be. After high school, I played in college at Louisiana Tech for a couple of years before turning pro at 21.

By the time I turned 24, after modest success I realized that I was meant to be a teacher. In this whole time I would help other players, and I got more satisfaction out of helping them then I did from my own golf game. My dream changed. I started dreaming of getting players on Tour, having them win a Tour event or a major. I liked helping people of all levels reach their goals.

I met Charlie King in 2003 and knew we wanted the same thing. We talked during a junior camp I was running in Tennessee and came up with the nuts and bolts of what became this book. We knew that even though there were thousands of books on golf, none had put together a program that a golfer could follow and get better for sure. And no book had put together a contest and interwoven motivation all the way through the book.

I have a reputation for being tough on my players. I'll tell you something I learned a long time ago. It's not what you know that determines your success, it's what you do. I will not settle for my players being less than they can be and that now includes you.

- Rob Akins

Don't let your ego, time constraints or any other factor prevent you from getting the professional help you need to play your best golf. Even the greatest players in the world have professional instructors whom they trust. David Toms is quick to share credit for his success with his boyhood friend, teacher and co-author of this book, Rob Akins. Jack Nicklaus had a lifelong teacher in Jack Grout. Arnold Palmer's only teacher was his dad, Deacon.

Having an instructor is not a requirement for this Challenge, although it is recommended. But even choosing the right instructor can be tricky. In this chapter, we'll let you in on the inside secrets of the golf instruction industry and with this insight give you a great chance to find a teacher/coach who can take you to the next level.

> " I will not settle for players being less than they can be and that now includes you. "

Not all instructors or golf schools are created equal. If you choose an instructor or golf school to help you succeed in this program, we want to make sure you pick the right one. In this chapter we'll go over the traits of a Master Instructor, give you a checklist for selecting a golf instructor or a golf school, and give you the eight interview questions you need to ask any prospective instructor.

One inspiration for this book was all the bad lessons we've had (the pain) and all the great instructors we've have been around (the pleasure). We want to pass on this knowledge to you so can be the passionate golfer you were when you started this game. Remember how great it felt when you first hit that perfect shot, or snaked that long putt into the hole in a crucial situation? That's what got you addicted to this game. We want to make sure you find one of these master teachers.

"For the next minute, I want you to think of the best teacher or coach you had in a class or sports. What was it about that person that makes them immediately spring to mind? Was it their dedication? Their knowledge? Their passion and enthusiasm? Did they care? I have asked this question for years in classes and seminars and the answer is much more about the subjective things as opposed to exact knowledge. Knowledge is a given. If this teacher is not knowledgeable, then you don't rank them. When I ask the people in my class or seminar to name the top attribute, I get answers like: caring, enthusiasm, sense of humor and the ability to elicit high achievement, to name a few. These attributes come from passion and dedication. The kind of passion and dedication your next instructor is going to have."

- Charlie King

Do not settle for less. Show him or her this book. Measure them against the traits of the Master Instructor, ask them the eight interview questions at right and see where they stack up. Take charge of the search process and then trust your teacher to be in charge during the lesson. You deserve the best. Period.

The Traits of a Master Golf Instructor

1. The instructor will implement a specific, organized program for improvement and not just rely on single isolated lessons. The program will include goals and a realistic time frame.

2. A short game skills test will be turned into an understandable short game handicap.

3. Your equipment will be checked to make sure you have, at the very least, the proper lie angle, shaft length and shaft flex.

4. The student will receive a set of basic stretching exercises.

5. The instructor will check for physical limitations.

6. There will be an equal emphasis on the short game and the full swing.

7. The instructor will teach the game of golf, not just the swing. This includes the mental side, course management, speed of play, rules and etiquette.

8. The instructor explains and demonstrates concepts in an understandable manner and in bite-size pieces. Information overload is not an issue.

9. The student will receive drills and/or training aids that will help turn these concepts into habits.

10. The instructor will use video analysis as a feedback tool. When used properly, video is a huge help in bridging the gap between fact and feel.

11. The instructor will convey a passion for the game of golf.

8 Interview Questions to ask a Prospective Instructor

1. How long have you been teaching?
2. Do you teach full-swing and short game equally?
3. Are you willing to help me follow the Athlon Red Zone Challenge?
4. What do you charge and do you give a break to those who sign up for a series of lessons?
5. Could you sum up your teaching philosophy for me?
6. Do you stand behind your work with a guarantee?
7. Will you let me do a trial lesson with you to make sure we are compatible?
8. Is there a wait to get a lesson with you?

8 Interview Questions to ask
Before Attending a Golf School

1. Do they show they care if you get better by having a follow-up program after you leave?

2. How many years of experience will the instructor assigned to you have?

3. Is this a serious golf school that is focused on making you better? Or is their belief, "People don't get better, this is just a nice vacation?"

4. What is the student to teacher ratio? (Don't settle for anything higher than four-to-one).

5. Is there at least one afternoon of an instructor on the golf course with you?

6. How many total hours of instruction will you receive, and how many of those are short game?

7. What is the teaching philosophy in 25 words or less?

8. How many rounds of golf are included?

We put this section in the book to give you some guidelines to help you make an informed choice. We hold ourselves to high standards and we want you to pick someone with high standards to help you with your game.

11

THE PSYCHOLOGY OF
A GREAT SHORT GAME

TO PARAPHRASE YOGI BERRA,

90 percent of golf is half-mental. Or something like that. I think what the oh-so-wise Berra was going for was this: Controlling your nerves and your emotions is critical to success in any sport — especially golf.

If you allow one of us to be your coach, you are giving us permission to do what we know to be necessary for you to reach the outer limits of your potential. The great moments of an athlete's life are those moments, win or lose, when that person has earned the inner pride and respect of knowing they gave it their all. At that moment you have a glimpse of your life's potential. Golf mirrors life in integrity and the emotional and psychological maturity it takes to succeed. This chapter offers advanced, yet simple information on how to condition your nervous system for success in golf and life.

When I met Rob Akins, I knew there was something different about his approach to teaching golf. Rob had a weeklong summer camp for 24 junior players ranging in age from 12 to 17. A mutual friend had arranged for me to be one of the teachers for the week. I was interested in spending some time with Rob on the lesson tee, so I agreed. In that week I saw some of the most unorthodox (by golf standards) techniques of any teacher I had been around. Rob alternately yelled, whispered, provoked and massaged the ego of the junior he was working with depending on what he felt the situation called for. I mention this to you because we have all been told how mental golf is. We see advice that is typically rooted in being nice to yourself and positive. But when we are honest with ourselves, we realize that many times it was the person who was willing to tell us the truth who influenced us the most. We have to know that the person cares.

> **The great moments of an athlete's life are those moments, win or lose, when that person has earned the inner pride and respect of knowing they gave it their all.**

For this junior week we would stay up late preparing for the next day by reviewing each junior's swing and getting on the same page about our instruction. Rob cares enough to prepare and he cares enough to tell the truth. In this chapter I want to give you a flavor of what you would get in a lesson with Rob, along with some tried and true information that I feel I can simplify for you to conquer the mental side.

That week planted the seed that led to this book. Rob was putting together a way of measuring the short game, handicapping it and setting a program for improvement. When I told him I already had done that and we had a similar desire to give golfers 'real' information that would lead to real improvement, the Red Zone was on its way. After meeting Rob, I wanted to bring his unique brand of golf instruction and motivation to you. What follows is an interview I did with Rob about his approach to reaching his players. It is 'real' and at times raw, but I can tell you in my 16 years of teaching, I haven't seen anyone motivate the way Rob does. The information in this book tied with this chapter on our motivation techniques will give you a complete idea of how to take your game to the next level.

- Charlie King

Rob Akins on Psychology

Warning: Don't Read This Section Unless You Can Handle the Truth

Charlie King sat down with Rob Akins and captured Rob's thoughts on motivation, mental toughness and what is required to develop a proper mindset for golf. Rob's comments are recorded below.

On how he's different from other teachers:

I don't look at their golf swings first. I ask questions and I look into their eyes to see what they are afraid of. Fear is at the root of our

mental struggles on the golf course. You've got to understand what you are afraid of. To improve on the golf course you must practice to make skills better and you MUST face your fear. This is at the heart of whether you can take your changes from the range to the course.

I apply pressure during most lessons. I need to know what you can take and what you can't. My players are _____ aments because I simulate tournament _____ by other players, I become that other play-_____ up as you swing or putt. If you're afraid of hit-_____ in the water, I take you to a pond or lake and we knock a few _____ on purpose. Hell, it's no big deal. You're still alive. It's just golf. _____ the game. Compete.

Put Yourself in the Game

_____ ant to tell you a story that is one of my favorites.

_____ n 1958, a young sophomore football player began the season as _____ third-string quarterback. It looked like he would have to wait his turn. In the opening game against Texas, Georgia was losing in the third quarter, 7–0, and the offense had stalled again. While the coach watched, frustrated, from the sideline, the young man walked over to him and pleaded, "Let me go in. I can move the team."

The coach didn't say a thing. Then Georgia regained possession, and this time the young quarterback did not ask to play again. He just ran onto the field, pretending not to hear the coach yelling at him to get off the field. It was too late for the coach to stop him. Fran Tarkenton went on to move Georgia 95 yards to a touchdown. After the two-point conversion, his team led 8–7.

I'm not sure if we would have known who Fran Tarkenton was if he had not been bold enough to put himself in the game. He was too small, and his college coach didn't think he would make it in the pros. How many limitations do people tell you that you have? Are you ready to overcome any perceived weaknesses? Fran Tarkenton boldly put himself into the game and I want you to do the same thing in golf: Put Yourself in the Game.

During a Lesson, I'm in Charge

One time a very successful multi-millionaire flew in from the West Coast to see me. I was running behind schedule, because I don't teach by what the clock says. I teach by when we have accomplished what we set out to accomplish. This man was obviously upset and he told me, "In my business all our meetings start on time." I had to set him

straight, "Listen, you flew two thousand miles to see me. I didn't fly two thousand miles to see you. This is my office and my business. I treat every lesson the same. When we start, I see what you need and we are going to stay here until it happens. To hell with who's next in line. All of my players know this. If you have to wait, tough."

I'll say it again: The range is my office. I'm in charge. I know what's best for your golf game. If the player thinks they know more than I do, they shouldn't come to see me.

On why he's constantly booked despite his unorthodox methods:

A lot of times I'm the only one in a person's life willing to tell them the truth. Nobody likes criticism, even if it's called constructive criticism. I tell my players the truth because I care just like I care for my own kids. That's what comes across at the end of the day. Most people have been told what they want to hear for so long, they start to believe it. I've got to create a belief system that brings out the best in a player. We don't always like the truth, but we respect it.

The end result is self-esteem. I feel I have a great chance to make a difference in my players' lives. So I ask them a question, "How good are you?" I usually get a deer-in-the-headlights look from the player. People don't want to be wrong, so they say, "I don't know."

So I ask a little bit differently, "Who are you, really?" I then get various answers about "I am the son of ..." or "I want to be the best player I can be."

I then tell them, "I know exactly who you are."

"Who's that?" they normally respond.

"Isn't that funny — I know who you are and you don't?"

"Okay, tell me."

"You are whatever you deeply believe you are. No more and no less."

My players usually respond with "What do you mean?" An
[ex]ample I give is if you believe you are a great putter, you will go to
[gr]eat lengths to prove it. After one bad putting day, you will con-
[si]der it a fluke. After two bad showings, you will practice and check
[th]e fundamentals that made you great and maybe see your teacher.
[Yo]u will not stand for bad putting if you believe you're great.

Tiger is the best because he believes he's the best. The willpower
[he] showed in 2004 to make cuts while he was struggling with his
[sw]ing change is truly amazing.

How many of us have
gone out and hit it good and
putted bad or hit it bad and
putted good and came up
with the same score? There's
a thermostat inside our head
that finds a way to make our
beliefs about ourselves true.
Do we leave any doubt with
our kids that they will learn to
walk? Hell, no. We praise
them for trying when they
fall down. We do whatever it
takes to help them overcome
[th]eir fear of falling and hurting themselves. We are patient and we
[d]on't give up on our kids because they don't get it right the first time.
[H]ow many of you have given up too quickly?

The reason we practice is to prove the belief that is being devel-
[o]ped. You don't just think it. You start to see it. In this age-old chick-
[e]n-or-the-egg question, I say it is the original belief in yourself that
[w]ill get the practice to be more productive and mean something.

I'll give you an example. I go lift weights and I know that I can
[b]ench-press 200 pounds, but I've never been able to lift more than
[2]00 pounds. Sure enough, I try to lift more and I can't do it. The
[n]ext time I work out, my workout partner slips an extra 10 pounds
[o]n there to make it 210. I think I've got 200 pounds on there so I
[fi]nd a way to get it up. This is the power of belief. You will find a
[w]ay to make your deeply-held belief come true.

Here's a story I heard that illustrates what we've been talking
[a]bout. Inside all of us is a white dog and a black dog. The white dog
[is] what is good about us — the honesty, morals and beliefs for a com-
[p]elling future. The black dog is our dark side — the doubts, fears,
[a]nd dark thoughts inside of us. The dog that is the strongest is the
[o]ne you feed the most. Are you feeding the white dog with strong
[b]eliefs and great practice habits or are you feeding that black dog with
[d]oubts and excessive anger? The one thing I haven't told you: The
[b]lack dog is stronger. He will eat the white dog if you don't feed the
[w]hite dog. If you feed the white dog, the black dog will always be
[t]here, but you can keep him at bay.

Three Buckets

I believe in life we have three buckets — one large, one medium
and one small. The large bucket has rocks. These rocks include your
moral character, your faith, honesty, integrity and love. The medium bucket has pebbles. These pebbles include your family, friends,
job and community. The small bucket has sand. The sand includ[es]
wealth, fame, recognition, jewelry and cars.

A person striving for the bucket of sand first cannot fit the pe[b]-
bles and rocks in their bucket. They are destined for emptiness. [A]
person striving for the bucket of pebbles can fit the sand but not th[e]
rocks. This person is happier but knows there is something missing[.]
A person striving for the bucket of rocks can fit the pebbles and th[e]
sand in his bucket. This is where fulfillment comes from. This person can have it all because they started with the bucket of rocks as
their foundation.

In golf, your bucket of rocks includes your identity, belief syste[m]
and work ethic. Your bucket of pebbles includes your puttin[g]
stroke, short game skills and golf swing fundamentals. Your bucke[t]
of sand includes birdies, pars, trophies and money. Take care [of]
golf's rocks before you can expect the pebbles and sand to fit in t[he]
bucket.

I'm Go[ing]

Whe[n]
over[...]
you[...]
say it[...]ove[...]
"I'm go[ing...]
what I've been [t]old,
human mind cannot th[ink]
positively and negative[ly]
the same time. If you kee[p]
that thought as you get [up]
to putt, you will have th[e cer]-
tainty it takes to make a c[on]-
fident stroke.

A Kid's Grades

I work with a lot of junior players as well as having three sons.
Grades in school are very important, and it is always an issue with a
certain number of kids. When I have a junior player who is struggling with grades I will ask him or her, "What grades do you set out
to get?" When the answer is "B's and C's," I know where the problem is. I tell them, "When your belief is that you are a B or C student, you will do what it takes to make B's and C's. You are happy
with 80 on a test. You don't study any harder. You don't ask more
questions. You don't work at it any harder. If you change what you
won't stand for, your grades will change."

Guess what, golfers, it's the same for you. We develop a comfort
that is an identity of who we are. We're a five handicap or a 90
shooter or a 30 handicap. We find a way to make that identity a reality. Set your target higher and do what it takes to get there.

Charlie King on Psychology
Do you control your Emotional State?

Your emotional state is the emotion that you are feeling at any given moment. Some are appropriate for your best golf and some are not. Out of control anger, frustration, depression, and resignation are emotions that hurt your performance. You know that, but

have you learned what to do about it? My research on this subject has taken me to many experts, books and seminars. The information I present here has been primarily influenced by peak performance coach Tony Robbins and my good friend, performance expert Dr. Rick Jensen.

How do you control your emotional state while playing golf? There are three primary factors: 1) Your physiology. 2) What you are focused on. 3) The language you are using internally and externally.

Your physiology is how your body moves and your posture. Are you erect and confident or are you slumped and down? How are you breathing? Full, deep breaths or shallow breaths? What do your eyes show? Fear, anger, concern? Or confidence? The question becomes, "Am I in control of my physiology or do I let my circumstances dictate it?" Until we take conscious control of our body, we are at the whim of circumstance and having control is as simple as deciding. Think of a time when you were playing your best golf. Picture how you walked, stood, spoke. Can you do this consciously or do you have to wait for good golf to give you this physiology and feeling?

What you focus on and how you focus are critical to your peak golf state. If you picture a ball flying majestically toward the flag and landing within inches of the hole, you will have a completely different internal experience than if you entertain the thought even for an instant of the ball curving toward the water. Your brain will take the picture and trigger the emotion that is associated with that experience. You can also control your focus with brightness, color and sound, to name a few.

The language you use determines where your emotions are and where they are headed. Weak tone of voice, whiny voice, and weak words can take you in an unhelpful direction. Weak, impotent words lead to weak, impotent emotions and actions. Strong words like "I will ...", " I MUST ...", "Let's go ..." lead to a state of certainty and confidence.

Why is your emotional state important? Can you imagine Tiger Woods saying to himself, "I hope I pull this shot off" or "I wish I had better luck"? Can you imagine Michael Jordan walking into a game slumped and meek? Or Mike Tyson in his prime looking frightened? Or Jack Nicklaus saying, "I might be able to beat these guys?" Of course not. These great athletes were confident and unstoppable. They didn't show up looking for second place and their body and language showed it. In his prime, Larry Bird would show up for the 3-Point Shootout at All-Star weekend and ask his competitors, "Which one of you guys is coming in second?" That's confidence.

Do you have to wait for good results to be confident? Absolutely not. You will see better results in our 12-week challenge if you decide in advance to go through it in a confident, unstoppable mental state. It's logical to proceed this way. Your body is responding to the signals from the brain and vice versa. You are learning new movements and integrating them. If you approach it with a sense that you have already achieved it, then your brain will be picturing good shots, better scores and the satisfaction that goes with them. If you approach the process with trepidation, your brain is picturing the "What if's". What if this doesn't work? What if I'm just not good enough? What if I try and fail? These what-if questions lead to pictures in the brain, which lead to emotions. None of these emotions help the process. The process of controlling your emotional state through your physiology, focus and language not only helps your golf game, but are the same mechanics that we all should have been taught to have a more rewarding life.

Here are your daily assignments that will transform your emotional state to one of strength and confidence.

1) Control your Physiology — Stand tall with your chest up and your center of gravity strong. Plant your feet solidly at shoulder width. Focus on your navel and feel your ab muscles go one inch in and 2 inches up. Be like a linebacker who can't be moved. Feel strong and unstoppable. Imagine how Tiger looks and feels when he heads to the first tee and everyone can see from his posture and demeanor that he is the man to beat. Decide in advance that you are not only going to play golf this way, but also live life this way. This is a conscious commitment.

2) Practice the Ability to Choose Your Focus — Whatever you focus on will determine how you feel at any given moment. Why do some people cry at a sad movie? After all, you don't know the characters and it is make-believe. You cry because for that moment, you decide that the situation is real. It's real to your nervous system. In golf, you can create your own movie and the corresponding feelings anytime you want to. When you feel nervous in a tournament, your brain is entertaining the thought of failure and that focus leads to fear, nervousness and tension in the body. Needless to say, that doesn't help you perform. If instead you calmly focused on executing the shot at hand, you would feel strong and confident.

3) Choose Your Words — In your daily talk, are you using strong, confident words that mirror confident performance, or are you saying weak words that mirror your self-doubt? For example, don't say 'try'. It's either do or don't. 'Might' is replaced by 'will' and 'should' is replaced by 'must'.

4) Say it Like a Drill Sergeant — Drill sergeants take raw recruits and create a different belief system during basic training.

nt to change the voice inside your head for the next 12 weeks. Some
you may have a nice voice that says everything is OK, but if the
ice for these 12 weeks belonged to your favorite team's coach or to
drill sergeant, you would get different results. Think about Louis
ossett, Jr. from "An Officer and a Gentlemen" — pushing Richard
re to surpass his self-imposed limits. This image, this voice is
reaming at you when you think about giving up or not doing your
ily practice. This voice won't let you settle for second best in your
e and your golf game.

Think of this scenario. You want to do the program. It all makes
se, but you have questions and doubts start to pop up in your head.
hat if I don't get better? What if I try and I fail? Why put that much
ork into a silly game? The answers to these questions are not inspir-
g. Instead of these weak "What if..." questions, you hear a voice
at says "Just Do It." This voice is stern and demanding. You know
ep down you can accomplish a lot more than you are, but you let
urself off the hook. This coach, this voice won't let you off the hook.
is voice will say, "Get it done." You fill in the blank. You know
hat this voice needs to say to keep you on track and motivated.

Affirmations are saying things to yourself that you want to be true
your life. The problem is we don't say it with enough emotion. All
us are talking to ourselves constantly. We have questions that we
k, answers to those questions and a tone of voice that answers
ose questions inside our head. Part of your success in this program
the way you handle this internal communication. Take statements
at you want to become true in your life and say them with con-
ction and full emotion. Get your whole body involved, your facial
pressions, and the tone of your voice. I find the car is a good place
do this so you can let it rip. For these 12 weeks take key state-
ents and be your own drill sergeant for golf's basic training.

Do a Rocking Chair Test

A Rocking Chair Test is to take yourself to your 85th birthday or
yond and sit in a rocking chair thinking about your life. What are
ou the most proud of and what do you regret? For this exercise we
e going to focus on your golf game. How much more could you
ve enjoyed your rounds of golf if you had made the Essentials into
bits? What would 12 weeks of commitment in your life have
eant for the next 15 to 50 years of improved golf? Really picture
ur game 50% better than it is now and playing the upcoming sea-
n. The increased pride and confidence. The ease of swinging the
ub. More putts falling, especially the short ones. More distance. All
this can be yours by following the 12-Week Challenge.

12

5 MINUTES TO BETTER GOLF™ ILLUSTRATED

This is the cornerstone of our program. The consistent use of these simple, effective drills will transform your game. We have designed this part of the program so that most of the exercises can be done indoors at home or in a hotel room. It will be the quality and consistency of your practice that will build the habits you need for Red Zone proficiency and give you a chance to be one of our future success stories. Five minutes a day per drill is all it takes.

1) Your Credit Card Can Make You Money

A: Find yourself a straight-on 8-foot putt. Once you think you've lined up correctly, have your buddy replace the ball with a credit card. The card will tell you the exact direction your putter face is pointing. **B/C**: Place the ball on top of the card, and putt.

2) The Arc Board

By allowing the putter to follow the slightly tilted board, you create the feel for a perfect path.

3) Right Hand Only

When putting with one hand, golfers naturally swing the putter and don't guide the ball. This leads to a sense of truly rolling the ball and not over-controlling and guiding it.

4) Look at the Hole

One of our favorites. This drill is simple. Instead of looking at the ball as you putt, look at the hole. Free-throw shooters don't focus on the ball; they look at the hoop. Like basketball and other sports where you get a good sense of the target by looking at it, the same thing happens in your putting. After the first few awkward putts, most golfers notice they develop an uncanny sense of speed and direction. Golfers have an innate sense of touch; they simply need something to draw it out of them. This drill does it.

5) Putting Mat

Watching the ball go in and creating a pattern of success is the key to the putting mat. Many of these drills should be adapted to the mat.

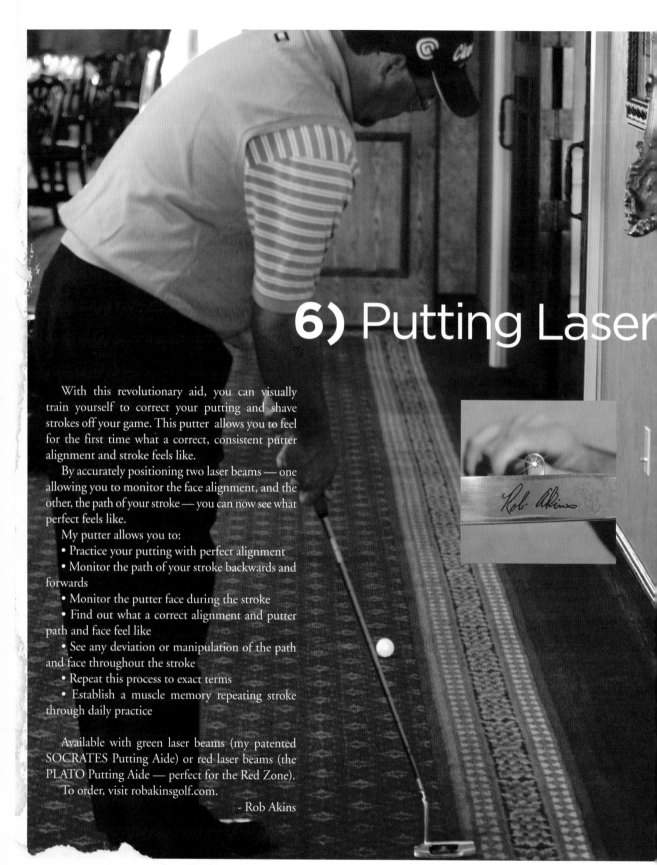

6) Putting Laser

With this revolutionary aid, you can visually train yourself to correct your putting and shave strokes off your game. This putter allows you to feel for the first time what a correct, consistent putter alignment and stroke feels like.

By accurately positioning two laser beams — one allowing you to monitor the face alignment, and the other, the path of your stroke — you can now see what perfect feels like.

My putter allows you to:
• Practice your putting with perfect alignment
• Monitor the path of your stroke backwards and forwards
• Monitor the putter face during the stroke
• Find out what a correct alignment and putter path and face feel like
• See any deviation or manipulation of the path and face throughout the stroke
• Repeat this process to exact terms
• Establish a muscle memory repeating stroke through daily practice

Available with green laser beams (my patented SOCRATES Putting Aide) or red laser beams (the PLATO Putting Aide — perfect for the Red Zone).
To order, visit robakinsgolf.com.

- Rob Akins

Take the club you are chipping with, then take another club out of your bag and turn it over and hold the two clubs so the upside down club sticks out beside your left hip. When you chip the ball the goal is for the upside down club not to hit you in the side. If you scoop and the club hits you, that is your "punishment."

7) The Punisher Club

8) Ping Pong Ball

You can use this drill inside. Hit chip shots with a ping pong ball. Notice how hitting slightly down makes the ball go up and puts some spin on the ball. Be creative and take what you learn to the real ball. I have all my juniors and many of my adult players use this drill indoors. This drill teaches my players touch, the effects of spin and imagination. It also helps you develop your intuition when chipping - that's critically important. I used to chip ping pong balls onto my dining room table at home and try to get them to stay there. It's a fun, competitive little game to play with a partner, and one that really helps you learn to shape your shots. And while you've got the ping pong balls out, experiment with them. See what it takes to make them curve. Hit draws and fades. You can easily pick up little habits to take with you to the course.

-Rob Akins

2) To square the face

3) To support the club at the top

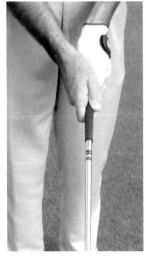

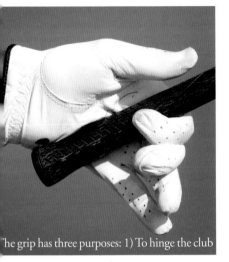

The grip has three purposes: 1) To hinge the club

Grip

The grip has three purposes: 1) to hinge the club, 2) square the face, and 3) give support at the top of the swing.

First, to correctly hinge the club, you should take the grip-end of the club and hold it only with the heel pad (which is placed on top the grip) and the forefinger. You should then move the club up and down to check if the club is hinged properly. When you wrap your remaining three fingers around the club, you should see two or three knuckles on their left hand. If you see four knuckles, the grip is too wrong; if you see no knuckles or just one knuckle, then the grip is too weak.

Next, you should place your right hand on the side of the club.

The way you put your hands on the club allows you to achieve the second function of the grip, which is to square the clubface.

Now, take the club to the top of your backswing. Your left thumb and the pad of your right forefinger should support the club. If you e doing this with your grip, you now have a correct, functional grip.

There is a misunderstanding about light grip pressure. We like to see that the pressure in the arms and wrists is light and the fingers are ug on the club. This gives us the best of both worlds: speed from light arm and wrist pressure and support of the club through snug fin-rs on the club.

Aim

Many players set up with their shoulders lined up to the target. This is another one of golf's misconceptions because, in reality, the player is now lined up to the right of the target. Because the clubface hits the ball, it only makes sense that you should line up your clubface with the target. A key principle to remember when going through your pre-shot routine is "clubface first, body second." Another key concept to remember is the shoulders are lined up parallel to and left of the target. The lower body should be lined up slightly to create resistance for the backswing. This resistance creates a stopping point. Because players are standing sideways and dealing with visual distortion, it takes practice and feedback to become good at alignment.

Posture

Why is good posture important? Because bad posture has three devastating effects: It restricts your arm movement; it restricts your body turn; and it leads to injuries.

When you stand straight, the back has a very small "s-shaped" curve. When you have good posture, the spine is healthy, and there should be a small gap between the vertebrae. Between vertebrae there is tissue called a disc, which acts as a cushion. When your posture gets slouched forward, the vertebrae touch, and the discs get squeezed and pinched. When this happens and you take your backswing, the vertebrae are grinding on each other and pinching the discs. This happens shot after shot, for years. The discs get inflamed and the back pain kicks in. Eventually you are unable to play because the pain is so severe.

So how do we avoid this? Well, one of the main principles in the set-up is to bend from the hips, not the waist. If you bend from the waist, your spine will be in the unhealthy position we just described. You must also have a slight knee flex to keep your weight balanced. This will get you in an athletic, balanced position to start your swing. We check this by giving you the "push" test. Once you take your posture, we give you a light push forward and backward to see that you are centered and cannot be pushed over easily. This allows you to learn to "feel" correct posture and weight distribution.

When you grip the club, your right hand is slightly lower than your left hand; corresponding to this, your right shoulder should be lower than your left. This slight tilt of the upper body we call "secondary angle." This secondary angle should be maintained throughout the golf swing.

10) Pivot Drill

Look in a mirror and check your set-up (keys for set-up are earlier in the chapter).

a. While looking face-on into the mirror, maintain the slight spine tilt as you turn.

b. While looking at the side view, make your turn with your shoulders maintaining a 90-degree angle relative to your spine bent forward.

11) Circle Tilted Over

Take your Sand Wedge and start out swinging as if the ball is teed up at your waist. This will result in a circular swing that is horizontal like a merry-go-round. Next, lower the circle as if the ball is teed up at your knees. This will result in your circle tilting over on more of a diagonal plane. Now go to ground level and make your circular swing. This creates an attitude of a whole motion instead of so many parts and a great swing plane.

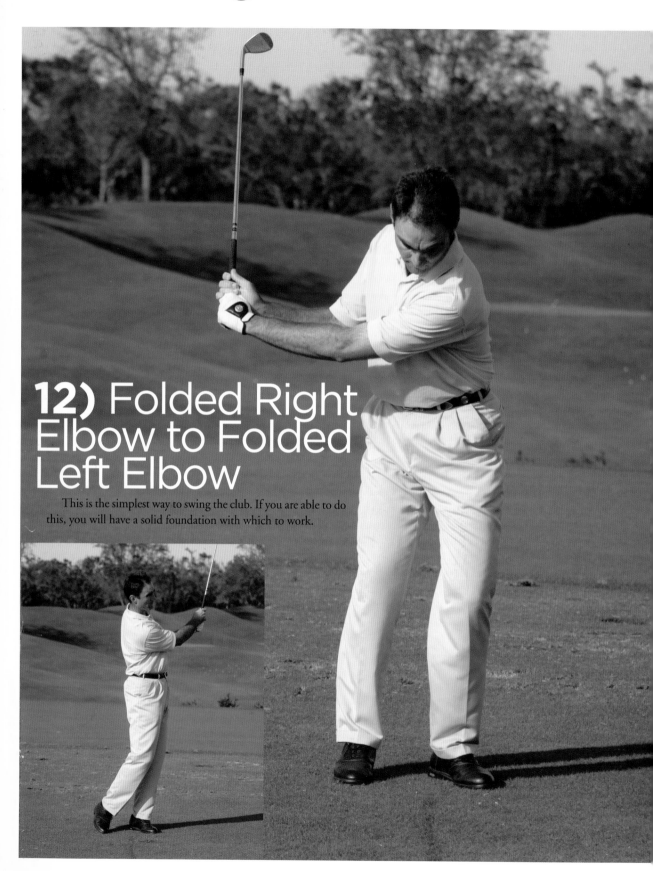

12) Folded Right Elbow to Folded Left Elbow

This is the simplest way to swing the club. If you are able to do this, you will have a solid foundation with which to work.

13) Three Finger Curl Down

The three-finger curl down is a great drill if you are scooping or slicing — or both. This drill counteracts the upward tendency of a Scooper and creates the downward hit of a Striker. Take a club halfway back and then start the club down while feeling the last three fingers of the left hand "curl down." As you curl the last three fingers down, the left wrist also arches out. This is what the late Claude Harmon used to refer to as "Bethlehem Steel" at impact. "You want to have Bethlehem steel at impact son, no linguine," Mr. Harmon would exhort. Do this drill as part of your 5 minutes to Better Golf™ and you will be on the road to solid, straight shots.

14) Hinge to Rehinge

Make a half-swing, focusing on the hinging and rehinging of the wrists. This will allow you to create maximum clubhead speed with minimal effort.

15) Line Drill

Draw a line on the ground with paint or use two tees to create an imaginary line. Make swings and take a small divot on or past that line. When you can accomplish this consistently, you will be able to hit more solid shots. If you are unable to brush the grass on that line, it is most likely because you are either falling back or bending your wrists, both of which are results of trying to "lift" the ball. Until you can consistently accomplish this task, you will not be able to move onto distance control.

16) Impact Bag

The best all around training aid. Pop the impact bag and you will see the hands lead and face square. Get the feeling that the bag "jumps" away from the clubface. Give the bag a healthy "pop".

Appendix A
RedZone Recommended Training Aids

We have assessed many training aids over the years, and our experience tells us that many times the simplest aids are the best. Below you will find the training aids that are listed in the earlier chapters of the book we have found are the simplest and the best. Consider the products listed below as your Red Zone Challenge Starter Kit. You can purchase these aids separately at www.golfaroundtheworld.com .

1. **Putting Mat -** This will allow you to practice your 5 Minutes to Better Golf™ drills inside.

2. **Stakes and Strings (or Pencils and Strings) -** This aid is one of our favorites and was listed by Tiger Woods as his favorite putting aid.

3. **The Putting Laser -** Designed by Red Zone co-author Rob Akins, this aid allows you to develop a perfect putting arc and face angle.

4. **Arc Board -** This aid is critical for developing a great path in your putting stroke. The Plexi Putting Track and the EyeLine Putting Plane are two that we recommend.

5. **Metronome -** This aid can be used throughout your game, from putter to driver, to help you develop rhythm.

6. **almostGolf Balls -** These are perfect for indoor chipping practice. You can also use ping-pong balls.

7. **Impact Bag -** One of the best. When you hit the bag, you develop a feel for good, solid impact.

8. **Essentials of Impact Board -** This aid is coming soon. Developed by Red Zone co-author Charlie King, this aid will allow you to practice the Line drill in your home. Check back frequently with athlonsports.com for its debut.

9. **Splash Board -** This board will help you gain confidence out of the bunker.

Appendix B
Charlie King Hierarchy of Skills

Starting with your putting grip and working your way out to the full swing is the best way to build a dependable golf game. In building your game, follow the order below; each subsequent level includes the preceding Skills:

Putting
1. Grip, Set-up
2. Clubface Angle
3. Speed
4. Centered Hits
5. Aim
6. Path
7. Swinging the Club, Rhythm

Chipping
8. Using a lofted club (Impact)

Pitching
9. Grip (3 Functions of a Grip)
10. Set-up
11. Hinging the Club
12. Width
13. Swing-Plane
14. Pivot (Body Movement)
15. Length of Swing
16. Connection, Timing

Full-Swing
17. Make same correct swing and length of shaft and loft take care of distance.

Bunker Play
18. Take a consistent divot of sand
19. Sand moves the ball
20. Mental Game and Course Management